New Poets
of
West Africa

Malthouse African Poetry

New Poets
of
West Africa

Edited by

Tijan M. Sallah

MALTHOUSE PRESS LTD

© Tijan M. Sallah 1995
First published 1995
ISBN 978 2601 98 5

Malthouse Press Limited
8 Amore Street, Off Toyin Street, Ikeja
P.O. Box 500, Ikeja, Lagos

Associated company
Malthouse Publishing (UK) Limited
19^A Paradise Street,
Oxford, OX1 1LD, UK

Typeset in Nigeria by Fena Typesetters & Graphics Limited, Amore Street, Ikeja, Lagos.

Contents

Senegal

Acknowledgements

The editor and his publishers gratefully acknowledge the poets themselves and the following copyright holders for permission to reprint the poems in this anthology:

For Kofi Anyidoho to Heinemann Educational Books and *African Commentary;* for Okey Ndibe, to *African Commentary;* for Ezenwa Ohaeto, to Delta Publications (Nigeria) Limited; for Funso Aiyejina, to *Okike*; for Odia Ofeimun, to Update Publications; for Niyi Osundare, to Heinemann Educational Books (Nigeria) Plc, Spectrum Books (Nigeria) Limited and Malthouse Press Ltd; for Tanure Ojaide, to Heinemann Educational Books, West Africa, Greenfield Press, Lotus Press, and Malthouse (Nigeria) Press; for Chimalum Nwankwo, to Cecta (Nigeria) Limited/ABIC Publishers; for Molara Ogundipe-Leslie, to Evans Brothers (Nigeria) Limited; for Phanuel Akubueze Egejuru, to ALA Newsletter; for Noel Ebony, Veronique Tadjo, Fernando D'Almeida, Cheikh Ndao, Amadou Lamine Sall, Yambo Ouologuem, to Editions Simoncini and Nouvelles Editions; for Tijani M. Sallah, to *African Commentary* and *Washington Review;* for Analla Gnoussira, to Nouvelles Editions; for Yves-Emmanuel Dogbe, to Editions Akpagnon; for Emmanuel Ngwaimbi Kombem, to Brunswick Publishing Corporation; for Silcarneyni Gueye, to Brussels Editions; for Kojo Laing, to Heinemann Educational Books; for Atukwei Okai., to *Greenfield Review;* for Kobena Eyi Acquah, to Asempa (Ghana) Publishers; for Abena P. A. Busia, to Africa World Press; for Lemuel Johnson, to Ardis Publishers; for Syl Cheney Coker, to Heinemann Educational Books; for Iyamide Hazeley, to Zora Press and Women's Press.

The editor and his publishers also gratefully acknowledge Faustine Boateng Gyima for translations from French to English of all the poems of the following poets which appear in this volume: poems by Veronique Tadjo, Fernando D'Almeida, Cheikh Ndao, Amadou Lamine Sall, Manden Wara, and Silcarneyni Gueye. The translations of the other poems from French to English were done by Fatim Haidara. These are the poems by Noel Ebony, and "The Crazy Heart" and "To My Husband" by Yambo Ouologuem. Translation rights belong to the editor.

Where it was not possible to contact poets or their publishers by the time of this publication, we publish the works in the hope of advancing the poet's reputation. We apologize for any errors and/or omissions in this volume, and welcome any queries or corrections for future editions.

About the Editor

Born in Sere Kunda, The Gambia, on 6 March, 1958, Tijan M. Sallah has been described as The Gambia's leading young poet and writer. He holds BSc and BA degrees from Berea College in Kentucky, and MA and PhD degrees in Economics from Virginia Polytechnic Institute. In 1984, he was among ten international poets honoured with an honorary doctorate by the World Academy of Arts and Culture in Taipei, Taiwan Province of China.

He has published three books of poems: *When Africa Was A Young Woman, Kora Land* and *Dreams of Dusty Roads,* and a book of short stories, *Before the New Earth.* His works have been reviewed over Radio Gambia and the BBC, and individual poems, fiction-reviews, and critical articles have appeared in *Black Scholar Callaloo, Kentucky Poetry Review, West Africa, Okike, and Presence Africaine.*

Tijan Sallah serves on the editorial board of several publications, including *Poet* (India) and *African Commentary.* He has taught economics at Virginia Tech, Kutztown; University of Pennsylvania, and North Carolina A&T State University. He currently works for the World Bank.

Introduction

That the new poets of West Africa are producing some of the most culturally vibrant artistic expressions in our contemporary world is amply demonstrated in this volume. The poems represented here reflect the idiomatic worldview of poets who all write in some European language (i.e., English, French, Portuguese, etc.) but who have skilfully mastered the interiority of such a language, imbibed its instrumentality, and domesticated it to serve their own individual and culture specific sensibilities.

This anthology differs in one major respect from earlier African anthologies: it focuses on the works of *new* poets. The adjective *new* is stressed because it is not uncommon in existing anthologies to encounter the ubiquitous names of such old poets as Leopold Sedar Senghor of Senegal; Wole Soyinka, the late Christopher Okigbo, and John Pepper Clark of Nigeria; Lenrie Peters of The Gambia; Dennis Brutus of South Africa; Kofi Awoonor of Ghana; and the late Okot p'Bitek of Uganda. Even in anthologies like Wole Soyinka's *Poems of Black Africa* or Gerald Moore and Ulli Beier's *Modern African Poetry* or the recent Afrocentric anthology of Chinweizu, *Voices from Twentieth Century Africa,* the temptation to succumb to the haunting dominance of these "old guard" of poets persists. The end result of many of these existing anthologies become predictable; they seek poetic legitimacy through appeal to the names and works of the old poets; hence the anthologies become works characterized not by novelty and uniqueness but by the recycling of familiar poets and their poems.

In making the current selection, I searched for poets whose works appear to be the most representative of the new and variegated scene of contemporary West African poetic creativity and life. Where possible, considerable effort was made to communicate directly with the concerned poets and to solicit their recommendation of other kindred-poets and their advice on editorial matters. Nigerian poets Tanure Ojaide and Molara Ogundipe-Leslie have, in this regard, been the most helpful. They made me appreciate the old African communal spirit of co-operation and the advantages of networking and teamwork in a literary enterprise. Editing this anthology was inevitably the experience of the "eagle on the *iroko*." Its success depended on the co-operation and efforts of other poets. Even though every effort was made to attain poetic inclusiveness, a few poets are not represented here either because of my unawareness of their works or my inability to reach them. They will be represented in future editions.

The title *New Poets of West Africa* conjures images of poets who are either young, or who, albeit old, started writing or publishing late; or whose works have been largely (and for whatever reason) underexposed. Many of the poets in this volume fit into one or more of these categories. The distinguishing feature of these poets (as compared with their "eurocentric" or "euromodernist" forerunners, to borrow a label from Nigerian poet/critic Chinweizu and his *Bolekaja**associates) is that they have been largely nurtured under the harsh economic and political environment of the 1970s and 1980s, a period of galloping inflation, lilliputian growth, structural adjustment, skill flight, mounting external debts, crumbling infrastructure, stubborn droughts, border conflicts, religious/sectarian clashes, impatient armies, and self-seeking *coup d'etats*. In such bleak times of destitution and deprivation for the majority of Africans, these poets have assumed the task of art for social advocacy in the hope of quickening the possibility for the attainment of a better world. Without sacrificing artistic integrity, they have employed their art to engineer purposeful social change. They are social gadflies. Poets with drums. Poets with spears. Poets with guns. Poets with bows and arrows. They are poets who have learned to employ the magical potency of language in order to radically alter the landscape of complacent minds and inspire them to fashion a more humane future.

The sources of inspiration of the new poets are both their local traditions and the works of the earlier African poets. Tanure Ojaide, the Nigerian poet and 1987 Africa Region Commonwealth Poetry Prize winner, provides a thoughtful recapitulation of what he perceives as the stylized tendencies characteristic of the old and new. He notes:

> New trends in modern African poetry are a development from and yet a deliberate reaction against earlier trends, especially those associated with early Okigbo, Soyinka and Clark...the younger poets who are highly educated and exposed are not as self-conscious as their predecessors. While they respect the older poets, they seem to reject their conservative poetic practices which are too formal and imitative of western poetic tradition. There started in the 1970s a strong trend to decolonize African poetry. Thus while one can fairly point out the influences of Eliot and Pound on Okigbo, of Hopkins on Clark and Shakespearisms in Soyinka, most poems written since about 1973 seem to have shed foreign influences.

Ojaide's observation is largely correct; tendencies in the new African poetry exhibit lesser degrees of self-consciousness and of aping European archetypes. But, could the ghosts of T.S. Eliot, Ezra Pound, Gerald Manley Hopkins, W.B. Yeats, William Shakespeare, and Aeschylus be evaded when most of the new poets write in a European language?

It would be self-servingly comforting to provide an affirmative answer. But the existing realities conspire against such a response. The very writing of African poetry in European languages poses a dilemma for the Afrocentric purists—the choice of language provides the. conduit for the influence of European literary masters on the African imagination. But this, in my view, need not be bad, to the extent that it is not unidirectional. European languages could be domesticated (so that we have an *African English, African French,* and *African Portuguese)* to serve the cultural needs of the African. They could also be used by African poets to influence the European mind, to*counterpenetrate*(to borrow a term from Ali Mazrui) the *northern citadels* of the European imagination. This, understandably, is being done, perhaps unconsciously, in African literature selections in stylized western curricula in the Humanities.

There are, of course, some African literati, such as the *Bolekaja trio* who champion an African poetics that is firmly rooted on African soil. This "return to the source" coterie of writers, often referred to as the *Bolekaja troika*, favour an Afrocentric poetic paradigm. But there is much confusion in their position as to what they really mean by an Afrocentric poetics. Does it mean a return to traditional African oratures rendered in African languages? Or does it mean that African poetics has to shed all foreign influences? But would that not be somehow unreasonable given that the very same modern African life reflects the ubiquitous and irreversible imprints of various foreign encrustations? Poetic art, we know, should mirror reality—as it was, as it is, and it should be. Contemporary African poetics should reflect the African poet standing solidly on his local ground but simultaneously aware of the value of relevant experiences drawn from other cultural universes. In his anthology, Wole Soyinka, whom the *troika* seem to have a personal disdain for,* expresses a much more consistent (if not also realistic) position than his detractors when he states:

> The excesses committed in a small part of the poetic output achieve an importance only for those who fail to see the poet's preoccupation as springing from the same source of creativity which activates the major technological developments; town-planning, sewage disposal, hydroelectric power. None of these...including the making of war...has taken place...without the awareness of foreign thought and culture patterns, and their exploitation. To recommend, on the one hand, that the embattled general or the liberation fighter seek the most sophisticated weaponry from Europe, America or China, while, on the other, that the poet totally expunge from his consciousness all knowledge of a foreign tradition in his own craft, is an absurdity.

It is an *absurdity*, if not an untenable position, to think it is all right to wear western suits and ties and ride western cars but simultaneously not all right to be influenced by western culture. Modernization is so much infected by western values and attitudes that to speak of modernization without some degree of westernization is as absurd as buying a Mercedes Benz and rejecting the German engineering in it.

Africa has much to learn from the West as is the case *vice versa*. Cultural autarky will not benefit either Africa or Europe and may indeed lower the world's cultural welfare in the same manner that isolation from the rest of the world impedes the process of cheaply acquiring useful technological lessons learned elsewhere. Everyone knows that the West, as we know it today, would have been deeply impoverished without cultural influences from Africa, and the reverse also holds.

In contemporary African poetics, what is needed is not the cutting of foreign influences but their domestication; not the preaching of hostilities towards alien literary achievements but the reordering of poetic priorities in the African cultural universe. Africans should make their poetics primary sources of artistic knowledge and foreign poetics as secondary.

In assessing the history of modern African poetry written in the European languages, one observes three distinct periods: pre-independence (colonial), independence, and the era of nationalism/post-nationalism. The pre-independence or *pioneer* poets of Anglophone Africa included H.I.E. Dhlomo of South Africa who published *Valley of a Thousand Hills* in 1941, R.E.G. Armattoe of Ghana who published *Between the Forest and the Sea* in 1950, Dennis Osadebay of Nigeria who published *Africa Sings* in 1953, Gladys Casely-Hayford of Ghana who published *Take Urn So* in 1948 and so on. Very much Europeanized, these poets focused their artistry on themes of race and racial pride; on the virtues of Christianity over traditional African religions which they referred to as *heathen or pagan* ways; on extolling the values of heroicism and patriotism; and on challenging European motives aimed at vilifying the African. Their poetry generally was dull, lacking imaginative freshness and imitative of the European models of their education. Biblical references, Greco-Roman allusions, mimicry of Victorian diction,, and metrical strictures, pursued for their own sake, generally decked the interiority of their poetics. In Francophone Africa, the poetry was largely dominated by the Negritude movement under the leadership of the pioneers, Leopold Sedar Senghor, David Diop, and Birago Diop of Senegal; Aimeé Césaire of Martinique; and Leon Gontran Damas of French Guiana. Negritude was essentially Afrocentric cultural nationalism caught in an infantile reaction to the French colonial/cultural policy of assimilation in Africa. It was an elitist construct set against the background of fragmented African selves searching for the hallowed water and glue of authentication.

Unlike their Anglophone counterparts, the *Negritude* poets condemned the arrogance of their colonial masters and their black capitalist allies, questioned the missionary zeal of Christianity, and extolled black values and the African past. Although they imbibed poetic techniques from the French symbolists, they generally sought their inspiration from the diaspora blacks and their romantic identification with continental Africa. The *Negrismo* movement in Cuba of the twenties, the Marcus Garvey movement, the Haitian revolution, and the Harlem Renaissance all provided a collective energy which was to find a celebrative reunion in the evocative works of the Negritude poets. Leopold Senghor defined Negritude as "the sum total of the cultural values of the Negro world." In this, he succumbed to the dilemma of a cultural ideology which espoused a specious racial/ideological humanism characteristic of groups with a certain internally cohering system of values and shared experience; viz. Marxism, Nippocentrism, Greek Hellenism, Arabism, Zionism or Sinocentrism. The problems with Negritude, as a self-defining ideological construct, became increasingly clear— it readily accepted, what Soyinka calls the "monocriterion of Europe"—the Cartesian thesis of *I think, therefore, I am* by presenting the African counter-thesis of *I feel, therefore, I am*—in the hope of arriving at the final synthesis, which is the truth of the "civilization of the universal." For Soyinka, this convenient European dichotomy of polarizing in order to understand reality misses the full existential picture. So for Soyinka, as with many English-speaking African poets, the idea of Africans proclaiming their *negritude* as a reaction to an implicit *blancotude* is the absurd product of the alienated mind. The African was not intrinsically different from the European; only that he had a different history. Therefore, Soyinka readily sided with Frantz Fanon's view that the person who worships the *Negro* is just as sick as the one who despises him. Hence, Soyinka's celebrated remark as to whether a "tiger will proclaim *his tigritude*" became timely; for it implicitly suggested that the less self-conscious the African writer was about his identity and the more natural he acted, the more he was to be taken seriously as a writer of enormous substance and integrity.

The independence era generation of poets in Anglophone Africa included Gabriel Okara, Christopher Okigbo, Wole Soyinka, John Pepper Clark, Lenrie Peters, Dennis Brutus, Kofi Awoonor, Okot p'Bitek, Kwesi Brew; and in Francophone Africa included all the Negritude poets (Senghor, U Tam'si, Birago Diop, David Diop, etc.); and in Lusophone Africa included Augustinho Neto, Antonio Jacinto, Vasco Cabral, and Noemia de Sousa. Some of these poets, of course, were also writing in the pre-independence phase and so do not neatly fit into iron-tight slices of time. But a dominant feature of most of their poetry was freshness of imagery; innovative use of language which remained sometimes sincere to local, flora and fauna or even to local deities and traditions; and utilization of African experience to articulate a uniquely personal voice. In some cases the poets demonstrated clear mastery of oral traditions (e.g., p'Bitek, Awoonor), and cleverly played with them to throw sarcasm and ridicule on the arrogant foibles of a transient modernity. Most of these poets, particularly the Anglophone ones trained at the University of Ibadan in the 1960s, mastered the techniques of Eliot, Pound, Hopkins, Milton, and Shakespeare and advanced them into the realm of personal experimentation. By the mid-sixties, Okigbo, and later, Soyinka, had peaked with their poetic experimentation to produce poetry that was vibrant, intense, and intellectual, sometimes to the "tent of even being exclusively *ivory tower* and *privatist*.

With the nationalist/post-nationalist phase, there emerged the new generation of poets, such as Tanure Ojaide, Molara Ogundipe-Leslie, Niyi Osundare, Ezenwa Ohaeto, Kofi Anyidoho, Syl Cheney-Coker, and Emmanuel Ngwaimbi Komben— poets who have been largely influenced by the independence generation of poets but who feel no urge to *prove something, as* their predecessors. They deal with their local realities with no colonial *hang-ups,* but with only commitment to their art and a sincere urge to see a positive social transformation. The following lines from Commonwealth Poetry Prize winner, Niyi Osundare, gives a superb illustration of the artistic achievements of the new poets. He sings:

> They too are the earth
> the swansongs of beggars sprawled-out
> in brimming gutters
> they are the earth
> under snakeskin shoes and Mercedes tyres.

The poet stands on the earth, informed by the realities of his environment, conscious of the existing social relations which elevate some at the expense of the marginalization of others. His position is empathetic and humanistic; he is able to locate his sympathy in the plight of the disadvantaged.

In the work of another new poet, Ezenwa Ohaeto, we see poetry that attempts not only to address socially relevant issues but that also utilizes socially relevant language. In the lines below, expressed in West African pidgin, we observe the employment of linguistic humour and commonplace images to achieve the energizing ef.fects of high art. The poet states in, "I Wan bi President":

> E get one dream
> Wey dey worry me
> I don dream am tire.
> ...
>
> Di dream bi say
> I wan bi President,

As if this bold wish is not enough, the poet goes to itemize why his dream to be a president is worth pursuing:

> I never see President hungry
> I never see President thirsty
> President no go worry for road
> Police no go stop-am for checking
> President no go worry for house
> Na government cook dey prepare food
> Na government dry cleaner dey wash cloth
> Na government driver dey drive motor
> Na him make I wan bi President,

The beauty of the poem is in the cataloguing of all of the worries of the *little person* and its juxtaposition with all of the excessive luxuries and abuses of the *big person*. In the end of the poem, the poet notes the excessive craze for *ego-massaging* which characterizes many a modern African president:

> I wan bi President
> Make I get plenty titles
> Dem go call me di Excellency
> I go bi Commander-in-Chief
> I fit bi-Field-Marshal and Admiral
> I go be Lion of di Niger
> I go answer Grand Commander of di nation
> Dem go address me as snake wey get forest.

My broda
I wan bi President
Even for my Papa House
But na dream I dey dream.

The poet uses the poem as a political exploratory device into the privileges and status-exaggeration of the Nigerian presidency but, in the end, squeezes his idealism to a realistic size. It is only a dream!

Perhaps no other new poet comes nearer to capturing the soul of the modern West African in their struggles against the predatory African state than Tanure Ojaide, particularly in the state's wholesale betrayal of public trust and its incessant, hard-nosed violations of individual rights. In his *Cannons for the Brave,* Tanure Ojaide paints a murky and brutal picture of the incestuous savagery of some African leaders in their aversion of the redemptive truths of public criticisms. As he puts it:

Shreds of intellectuals hang from branches of baobabs,
bones dissolve into the lagoon to assault us with bad breath.
We have dug up arms from distant farms
and wondered if the whole Republic were a boneyard.

If these sequence of images suffer from verbal hygiene, it is because the poet finds it hard to engage in hypocritical euphemisms in the face of state degradation of humanity.

The poet is pessimistic that increasingly *all the spear-tongued critics* are being *fed to roaming hyenas,* and what is being left is a voiceless population. This the poet perceives as a dangerous trend, for if the people cannot vote for their preferences through the ballot box then they should be left to vote with their voice. Increasingly, of course, many Africans are voting with their feet, as they migrate to greener pastures in voluntary or involuntary exile—a sad exodus contributing to the intellectual desolation of Africa. The cliché for this phenomenon is the *African brain drain.*

For Ojaide what is most disturbing about contemporary African governments is that they enlist *murderers or collaborators* from the presumed traditional bastions of morality - the religious institutions. For him, African autocrats have "enlisted assassins from churches and mosques" and "the long arm of state reaches everywhere and...has circled the land with awesome steel." The symbiotic bedmating between the shrine and, the stool have left little option for the ordinary African but either rebellion or weariness and despair.

This volume is, in essence, the voice of new West African poets shuffling through the many disguises that their surrounding reality takes. It speaks of all that is great and weak among us: the palm-wine and the shrine; the yam and the stool; and the aphorisms and the machetes. The poems blaze with laughter, solemnity, and rage. Self-criticism abound as much as "other criticism". Our continent is made to stand before a poetic mirror and stare at her blemishes. This anthology is more than a congregation of soul-searching voices; it is an intellectual celebration of talents shaping a coalescing vision.

Bolekaja: Translated literally from the Yoruba language means "Come down let's fight!"; it refers to the style of literary criticism advanced by three Nigerian intellectuals (Chinweizu, Onwuchekwa Jemie, and Ihechukwu Madubuike) in their controversial book, *Toward the Decolonization of African Literature.*

Tijan M. Sallah
Silver Spring, Maryland, USA,
December 1990.

Nigeria

**Osundare Ojaide Aiyejina
Nwankwo Ogundipe-Leslie Ofeimun
Ndibe Ohaeto Balogun
Ojo-Ade Garuba Enekwe Obadiah
Egejuru Biakolo**

Niyi Osundare

Born in 1947 at Ikere-Ekiti in Ondo State, Nigeria, Niyi Osundare had his second-
ary education at Amoye Grammar School and Christ School, all around his place of
birth. He later took a BA Honours degree in English at, the University of Ibadan,
an MA at Leeds University in the UK, and subsequently received the PhD at York.
University in Toronto, Canada.

Niyi Osundare has taught at several universities, including Wisconsin at
Madison and University of Ibadan, the latter where he has permanent tenure in the
Department of English.

He is a recipient of many honours and prizes, including *Waiting Laughters*
which won Malthouse Press Limited the 1991 Noma Award for Publishing in Af-
rica, Honourable Mention for the 1986 Noma Award for Publishing in Africa, the
1986 and 1987 Association of Nigerian Authors (ANA) prize for poetry, the 1986
Commonwealth Poetry Prize, the First Prize in the 1968 Western State Festival of
Arts and Culture, and the 1981 BBC Arts in Africa Award.

Among his many books of poetry are *Songs of the. Marketplace (1983)*,
Village Voices (1984), *A Nib in the Pond (1986)*, *The Eye of the Earth (1986)*,
Moonsongs (1988), *and Waiting Laughters,* winner of the 1991 Noma Award. Niyi
Osundare is also widely known for his able criticism and social commentary, espe-
cially as a columnist in the Lagos-based *Newswatch* magazine.

Ours to Plough, Not to Plunder

The Earth is ours to plough and plant
the hoe is our barber
the dibble her dimple

Out with mattocks and machetes
bring calabash trays and rocking baskets
let the sweat which swells earthroot
relieve heavy heaps of their tuberous burdens

Let wheatfields raise their breadsome hands
to the ripening sun

let legumes clothe the naked bosom
of shivering mounds
let the pawpaw swell and swing its headward breasts

Let water spring
from earth's unfathomed fountain
let gold rush
from her deep unseeable mines
hitch up a ladder to the dodging sky
let's put a sun in every night

Our earth is an unopened grainhouse,
a bustling barn in some far, uncharted jungle
a distant gem in a rough unhappy dust

This earth is
          ours to work not to waste
          ours to man not to maim
This earth is ours to plough, not to plunder

Further Phases XXII

Ikoyi*
          The moon here
          is a laundered lawn
          its grass the softness of infant fluff
          silence grazes like a joyous lamb,
          doors romp on lazy hinges
          the ceiling is a sky
          weighted down by chandeliers
          of pampered stars

Ajegunle**
          here the moon
          is a jungle,
          sad like a forgotten beard
          with tensioned climbers
          and undergrowths of cancerous fury;
          cobras of anger spit in every brook
          and nights are one long prowl
          of swindled leopards

The moon is a mask dancing ...

*   Ikoyi is a posh area of Lagos Island
**Ajegunle is a ghetto area of Lagos metropolis

They too are the Earth

They too are the earth
the swansongs of beggars sprawled out in brimming gutters they are the earth
under snakeskin shoes and Mercedes tyres

> They too are the earth
> the sweat and grime of
> millions hewing wood and hurling water
> they are the earth
> muddy every pore like naked moles

They too are the earth
the distant groans of thousands buried alive
in hard, unfathomable mines
They are the earth
of gold dreams and blood banks

> They too are the earth
> the old dying distant deaths
> in narrow abandoned hamlets
> they are the earth
> women battling centuries of *maleficent* slavery

Are they of this earth
who fritter the forest and harry the hills
Are they of this earth
who live that earth may die
Are they?

Meet me at Okeruku

Meet me at Okeruku*
where earth is one compact
of reddening powder daubed coquetishly
on the harmattan brown
of trembling houses

And when the rains are here
when this dust is clod and clay
show me your camwood shoes show me hurried toemarks on the ciphered pages
of narrow alleys awaiting the liquid erazer of the next shower

*a red-earth district in Ikere, around the poet's birthplace

Who says that drought was here

With these green guests around
who says that drought was here?

The rain has robed the earth
in vests of verdure
the rain has robed an earth
licked clean by the fiery tongue of drought

With these green guests around
Who says that drought was here?

Palms have shed the shroud of brown
cast over forest tops
by the careless match of tinder days
when flares flooded the earth
and hovering hawks taloned the tale
to the ears of the deafening sky

With these green guests around
Who says that drought was here?

Aflame with herbal joy
trees slap heaven's face
with the compound pride
of youthful leaves

drapering twigs into groves
once skeletal spires in
the unwinking face of the baking sun

With these green guests around
Who says that drought was here?

And anthills throw open their million gates
and winged termites swarm the warm welcome
of compassionate twilights
and butterflies court the fragrant company
of fledgling flowers
and milling moths paste wet lips
on the translucent ears of listening windows
and the swallow brailles a tune
on the copper face of the gathering lake
and weaverbirds pick up the chorus
in the leafening heights...
soon crispy mushrooms will break
the fast of venturing soles

With these green guests around
Who still says that drought was here?

Excerpts from *Waiting Laughters*

I

My song is the even rib
in the feather of the soaring bird
the pungent salt and smell of earth
where seeds rot for roots to rise

My song is the root
touching other roots
in a covenant below the crust
beyond the roving camera of the eye

My song is the embryo of day
in the globule of the rising dew;
a vow which earths the Word
in regions of answerable rains

My song is *Ogbigbotirigbo**
waiting on the stairs of the moon
garnering lights, garnering shadows,
waiting

*a large bird which flies high in the sky

II

Waiting,
all ways waiting,
like the mouth for its tongue

My land lies supine
like a giant in the sun
its mind a slab of petrified musing
its heart a deserted barn
of husky cravings

And in this March,
this March of my heated coming,
the sky is high in the centre of the sun
cobs faint in the loins of searing stalks,
the tuber has lost its voice in the stifling womb
of shrivelled heaps

A king there is
in this purple epoch of my unhappy land;
his first name is Hunger,
his proud father is Death
which guards the bones at every door

And the vultures are fat
crows call a feast at every dusk;
markets wear their stalls like creaking ribs
the squares are sour with the absence
of friendly feet

And Fat Cows swallow Lean Cows
and the Pharaoh who umpires the orgy
on the bank of a sniggering Niger
has neither wit nor will to wave a royal wand
The sages say his own cupboard groans
with a cache of glittering bones;

Just how can a soiled finger
clean its stymied brothers?

Ordinances tumble down like iron showers
decrees strut the streets like swaggering emperors
hangmen hug the noose like a delicate baby

and those who die thank Death
for his infinite mercies

Ibosi o *
Hands which go mouthwards
in seasons of ripening corn
have lost their homeward trip
to the waiting bowl
And yet corpulent towncriers
clog the ears of listless lanes;
praise-singers borrow the larynx
of eunuch thunders

The Desert marches in from the North;
the Sea sneaks in from the South;
manacles on their right,
on their left, chains recently oiled
with barrels of ancient treasons...

Waiting.

My land is a desert
waiting for the seminal fury
of uneasy showers

III

And the multitudes waiting,
all ways waiting,
in the corridors of hungry shadows

stretched skeletally out
in rice queues, bread queues
salt queues, water queues
long like a scarlet tear
from the short-tempered scourge
of the winkless sun

to the sprawling terror
of twilights of chilly hearths
an emptiness balloons the stomach,

* a loud cry for help

lethal like a blinding plague,

How many fishes will quell the rage
of this political hunger,
how many loaves?

The messiahs peep at
the tattered hordes from the paradise
of a Mercedesed distance

Their fences are high
their gates wild with
howls of alsatian soldiery

They too are waiting
for questions which find answers
at the back of History's book.

IV

Okerebu kerebu
Kerebu kerebu

And the snake says to the toad;
"I have not had a meal
For a good one week;

And my stomach yearns
For your juicy meat."

"Suppose I turn into a mountain?"
Asks the toad.

"I will level you in the valley
Of my belly."

"Suppose I turn into a river?"

"You will flow easily through
The channels of my mouth."

"Suppose I become one
Of your favourable children?"

"I will eat you
With all the motherly love
In this world."

The toad then turns into a rock
And the snake swallows it
With delicious despatch

*Ah! àràmòndà**
The mouth has swallowed something
Too hard for the mill of the stomach

Okerebú kerebú
kerebú kerebú

Our tale is a bride
Waiting
For the nimble fancy of the grooming ear.

* Wonder of wonders!

Tanure Ojaide

Born on 24 April, 1948 in Okpara-Inland, Delta State, Nigeria. Tanure Ojaide grew up in this mangrove forest and riverine area where he had his early education. He took a BA degree in English at the University of Ibadan, MA and PhD in Creative Writing and English respectively at Syracuse University. Tanure Ojaide has taught African Poetry, Creative Writing and Oral Literature at the University of Maiduguri since 1981 where, till recently, he edited a journal of literature studies, *Ganga*. He was a visiting Johnston Professor of English at Whitman College, and is now a Professor in the Department of Afro-American and African Studies of the University of North Carolina at Charlotte.

His several prizes for poetry include the Commonwealth Prize for the African Region (1987), the All Africa Okigbo Prize for Poetry (1988, endowed by Nigerian Nobel laureate, Wole Soyinka), Joint winner of the Association of Nigerian Authors (ANA) Poetry Prize (1988), the Overall winner of BBC Arts and Africa Poetry Award (1988), and Honourable Mention 1991 Noma Award for Publishing in Africa.

Among his many collections of poetry are *Children of Iroko and Other Poems (1973), Labyrinths of the Delta (1986), The Eagle's Vision (1987), The Endless Song (1989), and The Fate of Vultures and Other Poems, (1990), Day Dream of Ants (1995)* and *Cannons for the Brave (1995).* He has several works of literary criticism, including his recently published *The Poetry of Wole Soyinka.*

Love Song

The moon will be told of her beauty
under which we hide and seek our fill

Princess of Okene, there is balm
in every pore of your soul
Ebira Antelope, there is sleekness
to every step of your goal

The moon will be told of her beauty
under which we hide and seek our fill

Desert Captive, there is gold
to every soil you grace with your touch
Goddess of a new world, there is faith
in the songs of your worship

> The moon will be told of her beauty
> under which we hide and seek our fill

Spice of every day
Dancer inspiring the drummer
Song raising the voice of the singer
Gift of a lifetime

> The moon will be told of her beauty
> under which we hide and seek our fill

Your name is like your body
it evokes persistent freshness
I mutter the magic sound
for a vision of your full phase

> The moon will be told of her beauty
> under which we hide and seek our fill

Hunt of the Antelope takes me unscathed through briars
Sacrifice to the Princess opens me her bosom
Love of the Mermaid drives me to the sea of fortune
Worship of the Goddess transports me to the sky

> The moon will be told of her beauty
> the moon will be told of her duty
> we no longer hide to sing
> we no longer hide to seek

The Fate of Vultures

O Aridon, bring back my wealth
from rogue-vaults
legendary witness to comings and goings,
memory god, my mentor,
blaze an ash-trail to the hands
> that buried mountains in their bowels
> lifted crates of cash into their closets

I would not follow the hurricane,
nor would I the whirlwind
in their brazen sweep-away;
they leave misery in their wake.
I would not spread my ward's wealth in the open
and stir the assembly to stampede;
I would not smear my staff with the scorn of impotence.

You can tell
when one believes freedom is a windfall
and fans himself with flamboyance.
The chief and his council, a flock of flukes
gambolling in the veins of fortune.
Range chickens, they consume and scatter;
they ran for a pocket-lift
in the corridors of power and shared contracts in cabals—
the record produce and sales
fuelled the adolescent bonfire of fathers.

Shamgari, Shankari, shun *gari*
staple of the people
and toast champagne;
Alexius, architect of wind-razed mansions,
a mountain of capital.
Abuja has had its dreams!
O Aridon, bring back my wealth
from rogue-vaults;
they had all their free days,
let today be mine.
Cut back pictures of shame
for I know why
                    the gasping eagle, shorn of proud feathers
                    and sand-ridden, mumbles its own dirge
                    gazing at the *iroko*
                        it can no longer ascend...

Pity the fate of flash millionaires.
If they are not hurled into jail, they live
in the prisonhouses of their crimes and wives
and when they die, of course, only their kind
shower praises on vultures.

The Hawk prays for peace

After my feathers have turned red
with the blood of victims,
after I have converted the moon into a nest
and filled it with the spoils of undeclared war,
after I have seized the arms of the armed
and disabled the fighting spirit of the youth,
after I have become the only bird
and all titles and praisenames mine,
the sole proprietor of the world,
after I have become immortal,
let there be peace.

A Verdict of Stone

You fled this island in a bark,
breaking free from my embrace,
your soul shaped like a prow.
The island shrinks daily, the sea
closer by every step on land.

As I walk down the ruin of old blocks
into homes built on dead bones,
I know you were
Ayayughe of the tales,
gathering firewood after every storm
pounding yam for the little ones.

No doors open where you weaned
a dozen mouths who swung you here and there;
no windows watch the cherry-tree
(its fruits have lost their savage taste).
There all is abandoned
except the soil God keeps for His testament
And here I empty this bottle from my travels
over your head; the ocean deepened our love.
Since you broke faith with fiesh,
rags sewn to dress you,
I discern dirt piling and piling up
at the beach, the line between us.

In your flitting twilight, you called
my name with your last breath,

and I held you; but you were already
irrevocably possessed for the endless journey.
Today I call your name, *Amreghe*,
 with an elephant tusk;
the island vibrates with your music.

*Amreghe, the poet's grandmother who raised him

London

Your mouth has been a blade with which you axed away my pride
and reduced me to a manikin in your playhouse.
You robbed me at home, then drilled me with mean orders.
I have not only been the *Black Sample* to children,
but *Jimmy* to old women, a token species.
Now that I have come to you and seen you at your best, nude, what hidden
charms lies in your scars, moles, and eczema?
Cosmetics will not do for your body at your age, your face already subdued into
a bloodless stare.
For all your swagger, you cook with dented pots,
eat with rimless plates, scum-tanned wares.
You have not water to wash your face sour from inclemence;
your hearth is cold, and your family is dwindling.
The austerity at the palace is unprecedented,
and yet everything from a disused car to a castle is royal. You have become
sterile with age and misdeeds-
your past has caught up with you, and who
will bet a penny on your remaining year.
Your boy said he discovered the Niger, my lifeblood;
who discovered the Thames? Some Vandal drunk with war
fell into London's ditch with his danish gun
and came out to tell the world of the Thames.
You are ripe for a fresh discovery, a totem bear of the cold.

State Executive

Wherever we dug for safety, we dug into corpses
            - Donald Hall, *The One Day*

'Wherever we dug for safety, we dug into corpses.'
Whatever we hid in our guts, he found and wiped out.

Wherever we fled, he sent his deadly envoy to split us.
We could not shrug off this vicious head from our lives.

Shreds of intellectuals hang from branches of baobabs,
bones dissolve into the lagoon to assault us with bad breath.
We have dug up arms from distant farms
and wondered if the whole Republic were a boneyard.

All the evaporated faces found solace in the soil,
all the spear-tongued critics fed roaming hyenas.
Every year raises the chief's fund of machetes
winds smother wails and rain washes the topsoil.

From the beginning *Ogiso* chose cost-effective means
to exterminate the bugs that would ruin his rule;
he found beggar hands to implement blood without stain.
He enlisted assassins from churches and mosques.

For him the long arm of state reaches everywhere
and he has circled the land with awesome steel.

The executive wields Aladja-forged axes and rifles;
the human-hooded snake slithers to bite dissonant tongues.

Thousands of executions prove right his inaugural boast
of peace as an array of still bodies,
a cemetery with a busy stock exchange,
a record bloodpool chlorinated for a bath.

His rule a great safari of poachers,
a vast ward of diseased consultants,
a free market of limbs flavoured with cheap smiles
Ogres parade the streets in smart uniform.

Every day lingers with his infinite arm,
everywhere throws up freshly savaged flesh,
everyone yawns from the blood-laden air.
'Wherever we dug for safety, we dug into corpses.'

Funso Aiyejina

Born in 1950 in Edo State, Nigeria, Funso Aiyejina was, educated at the Universities of Ibadan, Acadia (Canada), and West Indies.

He is a lecturer in the Department of English Literature at the University of Ife (Obafemi Awolowo University).

He has published widely in various academic journals, including *Okike and Opon Ifa*. Some of his poems are in *Modern African Poetry* edited by Gerald Moore and Ulli Beier, and in *Rhythms of Creation*. In addition to poems, he has published short stories and done some radio plays.

Love in Ascent

When it storms
the anus of the chicken is opened for public viewing,
when the sun rises
it strips the night of its dark mysteries,
and when a giant river wanders into fragments
it dissipates its strength into the impotence of rivulets...

when dusk descended and made us apart
into pillars that stand each from each,
love ascended from between us
like vapours into the heavens
and abandoned us to the sudden pains
of truths hearts should have divulged
but contrived to conceal
until an uncanny wind came
and ruffled them awake into evidence...

thus silenced by pressurized hurts,
offspring of shock discoveries,
sworn friends become strangers to one another

and drift backward into memory lands
in search of pledges long lost to the source of water
of a river now grown too deep and too wide
for us to wade across, each to each,
as it was in the beginning
before we became estranged into separate beds
from where we contemplate worlds that flourish
only to flounder and fail
and truths that mock the efforts
of man's unending seasons of hope.

May ours not be

May ours not be like the story
of the Ear and the Mosquito;
but if it is, remember, o plunderers,
the Mosquito's eternal vow of protest,
for we shall become like lice
forever in your seams,
ant-heads that even in death
burrow deep into the flesh,
chameleon faeces that cannot
be wiped off the feet,
and regenerating earthworms
that multiply by their pieces;
if there is not rainbow in the sky,
we know how to create one
by splashing water in the face of the sun;
if sleepers' hands protect their ears,
mosquitoes must learn to bite at their legs
to awaken them into their broken pledges;
if treasure hunters disturb our Orukwu rockhill,
thunders will break behind our tongues of lightning
like arrows in flight...

After the last shot

(for Ososo, Dupe and the Future)

Does the fire that consumes the king and his palace
ever remain the exclusive sorrow of his household?
Where does the town turn when king-makers
demand the beaded crown and the staff of office

when a new king is found?
And what will the new king eat if not the old? '
What will he eat...?

> The child who overturns his lunch in anger
> Because it is not big enough
> Will surely know hunger
> Before the chickens go to roost.

Give us weight, the burden of the elephant,
to stay firm on earth.

The men that walk with their manhood
Between their emaciated thighs,
The dogs that stand with punchless howls
And frail tails between their hinder limbs,
The limp he-goats that tease the heated she-goats—
Whose masquerades are these
Whose headgears have descended to their feet ...?

> The masquerade that stays out for too long
> Always comes home with exposed toes
> And the crab that sleeps carelessly
> Becomes the doomed companion of the reckless flood.

Give us lightness, the pride of the eagle, to escape adversaries.

A water fall
Can it be a fall if it does not fall?
Can the music make without the falling water?
Unless the torrents tear through the checking craters
Can they ever descend to the foot of *Orukwu*
To water the baked farmlands
And open the gates for the promise of tomorrow...?

> Put past flames past your tender mind,
> The rods that catch *Sango's* * stray flames
> Can they ever catch the god himself?
> Become, therefore, the god's own goddess and strike
> With your pent-up love and emotion
> If this be the day and the hour
> For how many past heart breaks
> Shall we continue to recall
> And how much of the water of river Niger
> Can we drink before we die?

Give us weight for stability and wings for flight,
Give us voices for words that will not sound vacuously Like a ringing phone in
an empty room,
Let ours not be like the decorative front piece
That opens unto a filthy backyard.

But let us float
Above the smouldering flames of our time,
Let us float
Above the guilt ridden gales of our age,
This age of silent adults
And talking infants,
This time of public promises
And private retrievals,
Let us float
Like two copulating butterflies
Atop a midday heap of cow dung.

For except by refilling
How else can we make full
An empty bottle...?

Sango, Yoruba god of thunder

When the monuments to our legends

When the monuments to our legends
grow mossy with gradual truths
and our dew drops are hunted
to death by the sunspears
of our unrelieved summer noons,
we awake to the knowledge that
pond-dwelling pebbles cannot but
grow muddy with time, that rivers
will always gather the colours
over which they flow...

now that our messiahs of the greater tomorrow
have chased our dreams out of the sacred
corners of our homesteads unto the blind
alleys of our mangled ghettos and proceeded
to murder them before our wakeful eyes
summoning history as their witness,
it is time we reject those whose promises
are never fulfilled, who give us

only the barren fields, who have severed
the link between prayers and miracles;
it is time we learn to sing
songs of abuse for those who mock us
with numerous programmes named after us
but executed for the benefit of their pockets
and those who make us build the podium
on which they stand to salute our miseries
on every anniversary of the revolution.

Chimalum Nwankwo

Born in Ndikelionwu, Nigeria, Chimalum Nwankwo received his early education at St. George's School, Zaria, and the National Grammar School, Okigwe, all in Nigeria. He took a BA degree at the University of Nigeria, Nsukka, where he was one of the student editors of the *Muse*. Chimalum Nwankwo subsequently obtained the MFA, MA and PhD degrees at the University of Texas at Austin.

He has taught at the University of Nigeria and East Carolina University. He is presently teaching at North Carolina State University at Raleigh.

Chimalum Nwankwo has published several essays and reviews and, in addition, has to his credit a creative work, *The Trumpet Parable* (play), and two collections of poetry, *Feet of the Limping Dancers,* and *Toward the Aerial Zone.* The latter collection was the joint winner of the 1988 Association of Nigerian Authors Poetry Prize.

As to his artistic perspective, Chimalum Nwankwo has this to say:

While political neutrality may not be possible for writers, I remain wary of prescriptive criticism and unguarded fixations on culture, race and ideology. I find all extremes in life uncomfortable and unacceptable.

Bush Dirge

silence in the land of the living and dead
silence beyond the seven forests seven rivers
thunder blows from the heart of our silence

our quartermaster is counting our guns
why is the quartermaster counting our guns?
oh a white elephant has smashed through our homestead
ah let a black elephant smash through our homestead
but who can measure the clamour across the rivers?
who can measure the thunder across the rivers?
who can measure the thunder beyond the forests?
the people will measure the clamour beyond the forests
is it a clamour or thunder or a thunder or clamour?
it is the thunder of the dead above the voice of death

when thunder blows in the land of the dead
a hero has crossed the river in plumes
when thunder beams on the faces of the dead
a hero has joined the revels of our dead
when thunder laughs without tinders from trees
the living and the dead are sharing memories

now that our quartermaster is counting our guns
and our totem gleams with the spirit of the dead
who can recount a hero's last words?
thunder understands thunder is laughing,
thunder understands the falling leaves
a harmattan ritual before a warm rain

a funereal cloud before the festival sun
a silent colonnade before a fierce war
the little flower that drinks the morning air
the drooping petals will follow the evening sun
can a song of fire return a people's hero?

a song is a song the people the miracle
thunder blows in the land of the dead

who will remember the clan's next hero?
the people the people their memories are deathless
why shall a song blow for heroes at dusk?
their sinews are monuments everlasting fountains
how shall we make the next lines of our song?
there are no shores in the seas of the soul

remember the heroes the people remember
how can we remember the people's heroes?
from the skirmish to the battle the peak of our wars
from the crier's call to the thunder in the bush
from the little strokes the heroes felt in the fields
which rattled our homesteads rafters to eaves
speak again memory: blow with your thunders:
the women and cowards were there at the headcounts
with children they gloried like they did with kings
they drank at the square with the enemies' skulls no plumes on red caps no
gleams from golden stools
a ripe corn speaks from a husk of bronze

thunder blows for the living and dead

can or cannonade destroy the air?
a song of fire return a people's hero?

the people the people fire will warm our souls

now that our quartermaster is counting our guns
and fires glow in the bottom of our springs
fire in the hearts of singers fire in our hearts
let all the clan sing together now together

now that fear has fled from all our homesteads
let all the clan sing together now together

now that our quartermaster makes our guns
and the angels' feathers are the quills of our hens
and the devil's totem is the phlegm of our sages
and the corners of the courts have lost their secrets
who keeps his own guns will win in his wars
let all the clan sing together now together

thunder blows for the living and the dead

Poem

in sand
all the ostriches
had their heads

in their heads
all the ostriches
had sand

Eleventh Embrace

the eleventh embrace
has come my love and gone
now I must
peel my mask

and drop those words
that dog our dreams
like flaming furies
the spirit of an iron age
rests on the earth of our love
our automated bodies
talk without our consents
some sterile tears drip
on our protestations farms
oh what a harvest
fires and cyclones
of passion they burn
and blow them down those
little things that whisper
tenderly in the morning
of every love those little
songs of faith that keep
the ark high rising
in a rainstorm

To a lost fire bearer

I can tell
When my eyes close
when I need sleep

I can tell
This is not the season
This is not the season
Of head hunters

Whose stealth
Break the hyena's laughter
Whose lights
Sear my night
And bring fiery wonder
To my night
Of black velvet

I can tell
There is no boundary
Between
My bad dreams

And my waking moment

The hyena laughs
From horizon
To horizon

My night of silence
Is a hyena's laughter

Because

This is not the season
This is not the season
Of head hunters
When I need sleep
When I need sleep
I can tell.

Circles

serpents stalk in feasts with masks
blunted teeth have learnt in pain
daily one smiles at these strange cups
cold drops with wolves in ponds
we have looked to the sun for warmth
held the moonman's promises shut
we have seen circles swirl in the mind
we have tried to orchestrate their sways
we do not know who our dancers are
the forsaken dead or muddled living
we do not know who our dancers are
the ruling chiefs or charlatan princes
we do not know who our dancers are
the circles are the demons
and the singers their slaves

Lucky James

i danced with him to stupid songs
and pawned my head away
I hung a banner in the sky
and thought a world was built

he danced to hell with stupid songs
and dried his folly in fire
i held my banner to my head
and roared through barbs of steel

he laughs in hell the lucky James
he bought his soul with fire
i squirm alone and nurse my wounds
and feed on stones of grief

Molara Ogundipe-Leslie

Born on 27 December, 1940 in Lagos, Nigeria, Molara Ogundipe-Leslie is one of the most famous of the Nigerian women poets. She took a First Class honours degree in English at the University of London, and did further studies at Exeter College, University of Oxford.

She has taught at several universities, notably the Universities of Ibadan, Ife (Obafemi Awolowo University), and Ogun State. Others are Northwestern University, Illinois, and University of California. Molara Ogundipe-Leslie has also been a visiting scholar at King's College, Cambridge, Columbia University in New York, and a visiting fellow at Harvard University.

She is a recipient of many awards and honours, and is an active leader of many of the women causes in Africa and, indeed, internationally. In 1987, she was nominated as member of the International Women for a Meaningful Summit delegation to the Reagan and Gorbachev Peace Summits.

Apart from her collection of poems, *Sew the Old Days and Other Poems,* Molara Ogundipe-Leslie has published extensively in scholarly journals, and edited some books on feminist themes and women writing.

tendril love of africa

I see again and again in my eyes
the smile flit over your cheekbones
Reach like a tendril to caress your face
in those lean days that startled
do you joy
that life does not slaughter our dreams
our secret thoughts on its butcher bench of time
that we gather to ourselves
the scraps and bones of our dismembered being
hoard to nurse them
that death may not out-stare us?

song to black america of the sixties

(for hoyt fuller, sterling and elma stuckey)

when first I saw you laughing bigly
laughter at grief at the corners of eyes
when everywhere I saw those hands
skin washed pale around the nails
in buses, on counters, hallways and crossways
I saw Africa again.

I glanced Africa in those legs
standing proud in bitter quietude
puffing slight round duty shoe rime...
sensed Africa in those days
when you cleaved through stares
to sit at class
scorning nature's decay
seeking wisdom beyond years
fifty-five years old and a grandmother twice
I saw Africa in your pride.

I glimpsed Africa in your walk
leather-coat hanging
in dare-pawnshop folds
lean as a Masai
sculpture in motion
hat-brim tough, an *Oba's* umbrella
Caught Africa in your grace.

And those little sisters
coming in, helping out,
trying things, carrying on,
heard Africa in those smiles
in the 'how you doings'
the cravings for reach
time spent in love
in tensing joys
Bathed in Africa in those hours

Those days of yearning!
when all was talk of brotherhood
and sisterhood, renewed queenship
and renewed slaveries,

graves re-opening!
and dawns to come...

Rest silent yet, my images
rest silent.

Rest silent, for cacophonous noises rend the air
'Hey, listen, do you guys have buildings in afrikuh?'
'I am very bourgeois, yes, I don't deny
'I LIKE my frigidaires.'

I seek Life

(song to the United States of America)

I seek life
in the crevices of trees,
roots that touch, and
the flower's hidden womb.

I crave life
not in the cerebrations of conceit,
dry winds to soothe the battered self;
I seek life, in silences and acts,
self-prepared to birth our conceived selves.

To touch life
in the infant's grip; the callused hands
black-ringed around the nail; the boy's high laugh tremulous from what is
unbroken;
in ageing tremors, the coward's despair, the mind in flight;

here where life is bent and broken and beaten,
twisted and piled into metal heaps
I mother the winds of our separate fears
cradle the laughter that is taut between our eyes.

Cyclones of madness circle...
'Yey, man, to survive, man, you need survival skills
not history, shit, and culture'n stuff'
'You can get hung up on history, man,
and forget how to survaaaaaive.'

Educated re-plays echo thinly and Tomly
from polished academe

Towards a future without a past'
LET US BE
A truly unique people, the first, the most. . .
who dare, yes, who DARE assail the future
Without a past.'

I would not have you dissolve nor fossilise
for when our encapsulated spirit breaks its mould,
in its wail, its skin-pimpling cries, in the jagged
lyricism of our united acts, we shall seize Africa again.

Firi: Eye-Flash Poem*

I

mind's refuse heaped in flesh on life's roadside
lunatic at roundabout in Ibadan.

II

white hydrangeas bloom here in May
clustered showers of infant smiles.

*Firi: Yoruba adverb, meaning 'fast, quickly,' a reference to a 'fast movement.'

Yoruba Love

When they smile and they smile
and then begin to say
with pain on their brows
and songs in their voices:
'the nose is a cruel organ
and the heart without bone
for were the nose not cruel,
it would smell my love for you
and the heart if not boneless,
would feel my pain for you
and the throat, O, has no roots
or it would root to flower my love';
run for shelter, friend,
run for shelter.

Odia Ofeimun

Born in Edo State, Nigeria, in 1950, Odia Ofeimun studied at the University of Ibadan where he was a frequent contributor to the university publications. He took up political service in 1979.

His first collection of poems, *The Poet Lied,* became a collector's item in Nigeria because of its literary qualities and the public controversies it generated. His second collection, *A Handle for the Flutist and Other Poems,* though not as successful as the first, shows ample artistry as a work of considerable social merit. His first collection is generally cited as the beginning of the new poetry in Nigeria.

Odia Ofeimun is a member of the Editorial Board of the Lagos-based daily, *The Guardian,* and was once the General Secretary and now President of the Association of Nigerian Authors (ANA).

After the News

So he died. The Mogul. The bigman died
whose pears were ripened by disdain for his kind...
Removed from every sun and the friendliness of water
distanced forever from the fragrance of grass,
vegetal pomp and the lilt of birdsong
So he died. The warlord. The bigman died,
snatched from magic reeds and the chafe of flatterin wine
denied the gentle rout of woman's hands
and deserting his titles, his swaggersticks and his weighted beads

So he died. The rhino. The bigman died
after winning and winning the earth
with bulldozers and hooves of pride-gored gold
after reaching his gory fingers
into the bowels of rocks and the womb of forests
after conquering the lagoon and the stock exchange
So they also die who pull other lives by the roots
to make music from broken skulls

So they also cower with tails between their legs and fart

Like all of us (he was like all of us?) the millions
whom he counted only as fodder for the profit motive.

Like his factory hands who never got a raise
because the hoarded fort was booked, as always
for another bacchanal, another carousal...

Like all mortals (so he was mortal?) who did not hear
the thud of loot in their abject backyards
So he died, under the nose of his henchmen, his thugs
his talking drums and his praise singers

So he died. The bulldozer. The bigman died
unclenching his fist, spreading out to every wind
to the truth of an ancient wish and no wind
leaving his empire to the blitz of chance and locust
So he too owed the earth this last prostration
he too owed the earth this last prostration

A Serious Matter

We have no need for
the common salt of want and hunger
said the spokespersons of the people
as they rode kites of ballot paper
to the truth of an ancient wish

But we must stop these
air-conditioned arguments—
do something—said the People's lawyers
as they stood up and were
carried shoulder high

... when my mother came back
from the rally of rallies
the kitchenware welcomed her
with blank stares

The spokespersons of the people
did not tell her
where to find the next morsel
for her children

A memo to Papa

The mob reaching out
to touch the hem of your garments
awaits a miracle
You cannot wish away the dire torrents
the truth of their undoctored needs
you cannot run away now

You are hostage to the wish for totems
the road and yet the salvaged path-finder
You cannot wish away the emboldened visions
the dreams of glory pulled out of your fez cap
You cannot run away now

In the raveny of the simple equations
which gored and actuated your dissent
You may find that your egrets take wing as eagles
that our hunger exacts more blood than bread
But you must not run away now

Already, our pagan discontents defy
the olive branches that you hold out
for we are growing everyday into a fight
We demand life more beautiful than pictures
You cannot run away now

O you did not run away when
against the stubborn insistence of your jeremiads
the jaws of dungeons yawned deliriously
You made hope into our common salt
You cannot run away now.

Okey Ndibe

Born in Yola, North-western Nigeria, on 15 May, 1960, Okey Ndibe holds a diploma in Business Administration from the Institute of Management and Technology, Enugu.

Ndibe is a perspective and courageous journalist who is well regarded in his country and throughout Africa. Possessing sharp instincts and tremendous journalistic ability, he was able to rise rapidly in several newspapers and magazine establishments. He has been Associate Editor and Chairman of the Editorial Board of the *African Concord*, and a member of the Editorial Board of the Satellite Group of Newspapers, all in Nigeria. He has also published in several genres extensively. He is the current editor of the *African Commentary*.

Ugo
(a love poem)

The eagle conquers celestial heights,
the anointed acrobat
of the heavenly space

The iroko tree commands the heights
the earth's finger
thrust out into the sky's face

The conqueror of heights journeying
to the fabled feast;
perches, on a brief stop, atop
the earth's longest finger
The foetal eye stares
from the sky where the eagle heads
for a feast
with the gods

Prayer

Sun

Break out
from the hymen
of clouds

and let a cold world
know the healing heat

of your touch

Demilicracy
(or a dirge for a Democratic Fetus)

Again
The shrill sirens have
silenced the fledging fetus
conceived—
of the people?
by the people?
for the people?

The night's shadows are cast
over the people's unrelieved anxieties
But the finger
on the trigger
The mouth recounting
yesterday's felonies
in a stiff barracks' voice
The boots squelching
the civilian charade will
in time nudge us to
darker labyrinths -

For now, our allayed anxieties
overfed on sugar-coated promissory notes
will soon be betrayed when
our bloodied bodies and

broken bones
bear witness
to the vile deeds
of a bastard prince
weaned on a gun!

Old Breasts

...Breasts bowed
to the assaults of
countless male-cious hands
A skin creased
from concussion of
a thousand unreached climaxes
A hidden heart
broken by unmeant promises made
by men on heat
Their damp crotches captive
in her trusting, deceiving hands
Yesterday was her day
Today her death
Her men of yesterday
now flock after the
fresher faces
sheenier skins
rounder buttocks
firmer breasts and
agiler sex of
the new competition
And she of the wrinkled, bruised body,
lonely by her unsought door stares
vacantly into:
Is it the sprawling waste of a past
conceived in hope
and born into hopelessness?

Or a future that will yet
exact the harsh price
of a misspent past?
There is not for her the luxury
of Old Testament logic: the fathers
have eaten sour grapes

and the children's teeth are set on edge.
The verdict
is upon her.
Too late for her now.
The autumn of a breast-dealer
is a lonely widow's dirge
sung to a cruel void,
A time to take stock
of a life-long investment
that yields bastard dividends.

Ezenwa Ohaeto

Born in Eastern Nigeria, Ezenwa Ohaeto took the BA and MA degrees at the University of Nigeria, Nsukka, and his doctoral at the University of Benin, Nigeria.

Ezenwa Ohaeto has taught at the Advanced Teachers College (ATC) of the Ahmadu Bello University, Kano Campus. He also taught literature and English at the Anambra State College of Education, Awka, before leaving for Alvan Ikoku College of Education, Owerri, Imo State of Nigeria.

He is the recipient of many prizes: first prize in story competition at the University of Nigeria, Nsukka (1978) and the BBC Arts and Africa Poetry Award (1981), and best free verse poem in *Orphic Lute (1985)*.

Among his many books are *Songs of A Traveller* (1986), *The Hand of Wind* (1988), and *I wan bi President* (1988). He has a collection, *Pieces of Madness,* with Malthouse Press Ltd. Ezenwa Ohaeto is widely anthologized and his works occasionally appear in such publications as *Okike, Obsidian, West Africa, Ufahamu, The Literary Half-Yearly, Kunapipi, and Trinidad and Tobago Review.* He is developing a growing reputation as an able and prolific critic.

Looking at Lagos

We have known you raped
We have known you submit
To fangs of prancing parasites,

You pulled from comforts of villages
Men who flounder in pillaged dreams,
Quaking in Kaleidoscopic house of dreams,

Lagos, you wear lights
Glittering like fairy robes
Your hairs gleam and glow
With moonlights of the night,

No one gazing rapturously

No one flying in clouds above
Would decipher the painful sorrow
Lurking in your dense undergrowth,

Your weapons remain in man
the haste the hustle the hurry
the tears the moans the groans
the grins the smiles the guffaws
the lure of lucre the length of lies
the heap of hate the lump of love
For you defeat them all,

But then Lagos who owns you
Certainly not the prisoners
Yoked to the navel of your mirages
For you laugh leeringly at last
When they are subdued.

I wan bi President

E get one dream
Wey dey worry me
I don dream am tire,

If I sleep small
Na di dream go come
If I close eye small
Na di dream go come
If I siddon for chair
say make I rest small
Na di dream go come
I think say na malaria dey come,

For night when I lie for bed
When hunger dey blow me
When I never see food chop
When I never see water drink
Na di dream go come,

E get one dream
wey dey worry me
Di dream bi say
I wan bi President,

I never see President hungry
I never see President thirsty
President no go worry for road
Police no go stop am for checking
President no go worry for house
Na government cook dey make food
Na government driver dey drive motor
Na him make I wan bi President,
President dey go where e like
President dey do wetin e like
If President wan travel
Na siren dey clear road
param param piroo piroo
Every car go run comot for road too
Na Presient dey pass for road,

Dem go close di road
Dem go close even air too
Dem go take one car carry am
Dem go take another one dey follow
All dem vehicle tyre dey new
All dem vehicle engine dey new
Di seat go clean well well
Na President get country

I never see President walk ten mile
If e wan go give person message,
I never see President begin cry
If e no see motor wey go carry-am
I never see President push truck
From morning reach night
Even if e no find ten kobo chop,

I never see President go farm
With hoe wey don spoil finish
De day e dey plant crop for farm
Na him make I wan be President,

If you see President him servant
Dem body dey fat well well
If you see President him wife
She go dey smile as e dey happy
If you see President him children
Na guard go dey follow dem
Na special treatment dem go get

Na'im make I wan bi President,

President dey different different sha!
Some president dem dey
Wey no dey win election
Some president dem dey
Wey no dey lose election
Some president dem dey
Wey dey rule forever,

President dey different different sha!
Some President dem dey
Wey no dey win election
Some President dem dey
Wey no dey lose election
Some President dem dey
Wey dey rule forever,

President dey different different
Some President dem dey
Wey dey make ideology
Dey look like person wey no see food chop
Some president dem dey
Wey dey worry make dem country better
You go see suffer for dem face
Some President dem dey
Wey dey kill person like dem bi flies
If you frown face na firing squad
If you say you no see food chop
Na bullet you go see chop one time
Some president dem dey
Wey don fat like person we dey for fattening room
President dey different different

If President go oversea
Na for red carpet e go walk
Na so so salute dem go dey make
Na special aeroplane go carry am
Na for best hotel e go sleep
Dem fit give am special woman sef for night
President fit take cocaine travel too
E fit carry heroin dey go
E fit bring hemp return
Dem no dey search President,

I wan bi President like Russia dem own
If him sneeze every country go begin cry
I wan be President like America dem own
If him cough every country go begin weep,

I wan be President
If I wan marry beautiful wife
I go order make she come
If I wan chop better food
I go order make dem go bring am
If I wan girlfriend sef
Na so I go send driver for evening,

I wan bi President
For work no go dey trouble me
I go dey make enjoyment as I like
Person go write my speech
Person go drive di car
I fit send person sef make e go read am,

I wan bi President
If food no dey market I no worry
If dem say price don rise I no go worry
If salary no come on time I no go worry
If petrol dey cost too much I no go worry
If sanitation exercise dey I no go worry
If na religion trouble dey I no go worry

I wan bi President
Make people enjoy too
    Wetin bi federal character
Every industry go dey there
    Wetin bi disadvantaged area
Every appointment go go there
    Wetin bi geographical spread
every promotion go bi for dem
Federal character na for person wey no get broda,

I wan bi President
We dem go dey praise
Every street go carry my name
I go rename all university for di country
All di town go carry my name

'If dem publish newspaper or magazine
Wey curse me even small
Na bomb I go take teach dem lesson

If I dey pass for road
Every person go stand dey wave

I wan bi President
Make I get plenty titles
Dem go call me de Excellency
I go bi Commander-in-Chief
I fit bi Field Marshall and Admiral
I go bi Lion of de Niger
I go answer Grand Commander of di Nation
Dem go address me as snake wey get forest,

My broda
I wan bi President
Even for my Papa House

But na dream I dey dream.

The Testimony of a Lunatic

Soothing moments of meaning
Could come from songs of the rain
And the streets come alive with hope

The glory of a medicine man
Lies in the tattered hat
But where does glory reside
Since so much has happened
Add so much still happening

The Lizard will frighten a man
Bitten by a slithering snake
But as you blame the robber
You caution the careless owner

Let us reason together now
What other kindness
Is offered the dead man
Except quick neat burial

Listen
It is well the fowl carries
The corpse of the dog
For if the dog carries the fowl
It will be charged with its death,

I know
Useful ears do not
spread across the head
For an ear that will hearken
Feels satiated with a word

Some truths so bite the ear
That the eyes grow in surprise
And hypocrites shake heads
To indicate warped innocence

Listen to the biting truth:
A reckless hunting expedition
Produces an animal without a name,
A finger is enough for
Lovers to exchange thoughts;
Some truths so bite the ear
But we cannot overfeed the baby
Despite the depth of our lover

Where does the Rainbow Live?

(for KCN)

I

If the star in my soul is stricken
If the planet of my plan is putrid
If the moon in my mind is on edge

Will the sun in my eyes sink too?

Presidents pay obeisance
But who can swear
the unknown soldier was not a coward?

Soldier we know

flower that grew in thorns

I have graded my tears
If death must visit the clan
Let it take away only idiots.

A thousand years of sorrow
Swirling like mist,
What has it produced?

Two thousand years of wails
Have not added an iota to peace,
Auction the wails to the highest bidder
Before the heat of exasperation dries them.

An ensign has been hoisted
The flag is at half mast
The wind has come to the forest
let the leaves descend in respect.

II

Dawn strips the nightmare naked
Daylight obliterates the horns of the dog
The sun burns out the secrets daily

But the memory is confidential

Gratitude dies with time.

There is austerity of tears
Even the laughter is scarce
Inflation has destroyed
the economy of the smiles.

The smile has gone out of the laugh
    Only the grimace is left
The tears have gone out of the wails
    Only the moans are left

We do not want to know
the number of stars in the sky
the quantity of sand on the beach

But tell us
Where does the rainbow live?

They have set fire to the Niger
They want to burn even the single leaf left
Our shadow is now ashamed of us.

The petals of life drip blood
The scavenger squad is ready

The gnashing of teeth
        Is for the living skeletons.

The finger that picks the nose
Can scratch the anus.

What is beyond this maimed morning
What is beyond this nagging moon
Is it the nimble night of neurosis?

You opened the shuttered windows
You weeded the farm

You planted the yams
But they ate them in your absence.

The drummers are beating the same tune
The singers clear their voices for the same song
The dancers rehearse the same dance
Who will chase the fowls away
Now that the cockroaches are outside.

III

Let the praises be assembled;

*Ogbojuode!

Fire that devoured water
Your words calmed the volcano
Even the planets listened
Venomous snakes quietened.
 Crab that could not be eaten in secret

Hunter that tamed the leopards

Warrior that paved the forest path
When the waves tossed
When the storm raged
You held the winds,
Even the cyclone obeyed
Your palm of justice.

The lion fell
The tiger fell
The sheep fell
But you fell too,
For the artery cannot cut
Without drawing blood.

Dinner guest who left halfway to end of dinner,

No army bade you farewell
No soldier gave you last salute.

Assemble the praises

For the grass that you fell upon
For the earth that grew them

Ogbojuode!

The river has kissed all shores
The stream has fingered all tongues
The ocean has caressed all seas

Your memory makes love to our hopes.

IV

The town crier has emerged
But no one listens to the message.

The struggle is now
for the anklet of authority

The cacophony is now
for the crumbs of national cake

The stampede is now
for the throne of power

The oscillation is now
for the eagle feather of wealth

Expose our pride
Hiding in the treeless forest

Rescue our reputation
drowning in the waterless ocean.

The age of the river is unknown
Who can claim he is the elder?

The wind has neither hands nor legs
But it uproots trees

Is anyone greater than the earth?

The eagle feather will float away
the caps of power will tumble down
The anklet of authority will break

But who will open the windows again?

They poured faeces into the stream
Where shall we procure drinking water?

It is more than a decade,
Who will weed the farms?
The weeds choke even themselves,

If the rainbow lies across the sky
And it is the harbinger of heavy rains
The erosion may wash away the farms

Shall we then stop the rainbow?

If we must
Where does the rainbow live?

F. Odun Balogun

Born in April 1946 in Oka, Ondo State, Nigeria, Odun Balogun received an MA
Philology from Leningrad State University, USSR, and took a PhD in Slavic
Languages and Literatures at the University of Illinois in Urbana-Champaign.
He has taught at several universities in Nigeria and the USA, including the
University of Benin, the University of Illinois-Urbana Champaign, Ohio State
University, and George Mason University where he is currently a visiting
professor.

Largely known as a short story writer whose work has been widely
anthologized, Odun Balogun's first collection of short stories, *The Apprentice
and Other Stories,* is being published. A second title, *Structurally Adjusted,* is
almost ready. He has also published several scholarly articles of criticism, and a
book titled *Tradition and Modernity in the African Short Story,* should be out
anytime now.

Where the sun rises

Beautifully chiselled into Egg
The colour where
Black and White blend into
The East
HER FACE
Is where the sun rises
HER FACE
Where the sun rises glows
With soft radiance
Of dawn as day
Casts on you its spell
India
Where she was born

I met her at friends
Ever since, I have wished

There were no dusks,
So the sun could always rise on
HER FACE

But where we met
Is where the sun
Always goes down

Today I ran into her
But it was dusk on
HER FACE
Where the sun should radiate

I wept for dawn
Wondering
What/who had
Cruelly stolen the sun from
HER FACE
Leaving a pathetic dusk

Femi Ojo-Ade

Born in 1943 in Lagos, Femi Ojo-Ade received his secondary education in Nigeria, and had his university education in Dakar, Senegal, and Canada, obtaining his PhD in French at the University of Toronto.

Femi Ojo-Ade has taught at several universities in Nigeria, Canada and the USA. In Nigeria, he served as the Head of Department of Foreign Languages at the Obafemi Awolowo University in Ile-Ife. He is presently Professor of French at St. Mary's College of Maryland, USA.

A renowned critic of Black Literature, Femi Ojo-Ade has published several articles and books, including two on René Maran. A creative writer, his first novel, *Home, Sweet, Sweet Home,* was recently translated into Portuguese in Brazil. Apart from publishing numerous poems in various journals and magazines, he has just completed a short story manuscript and a critical text on the Negritude poet, Léon-Gontran Damas.

mulatto

(for léon-gontran damas)

give me
the sad samba
the racy rumba
the bouncy bolero
the raunchy rhythm
of my beloved Africa

rid me of
the racist rhythm
the wormy waltz
the civilized xylophone
the vile violin
of their france
of their spain
of their portugal

and the orchestra's playing that song again
esclavo soy
a slow trot
swing ding ding
dang ding dang
charleston
boogie woogie
boom boom bam
BUM

and slave indeed i am
of their civilized culture
messing with my mind
according me a borrowed body and soul-

afro-amerindo-european
titika titika titi titi ka ka
jive jive jitterbug
dom dom titi dom
dom titi dom
dom titi titi dom
do-re-mi-fa
you jiveass turkey
you made me
then you left me
dangling between + betwixt
cultures and civilizations
quadroon
octoroon
dongla
mulatto
mixed-blood
mixed-up
ka ka ka titi ka

ka titi ka
ka titi titi ka
so-la-ti-do
i get high on hypocrisy and hate
black is a scoundrel
black is a nigger

black like sunday
black like plague

black like misery
black like death
i worship white
cos i'm not white
or almost white
the man of the middles
in the middle of a white world
leading to nowhere

afroamerindoeuropean
NO
cos i'm finally free
free to live my life
free to love my Africa
so give me
that sad samba
that racy rumba
that bouncy bolero
that raunchy rhythm
of Mother Africa

diaspora

(for aiméé césaire)

(they dreamt of a messiah
white as snow
descending from nowhere
with a wand in his hand
and fire in his breath
mr. miracle man
mumbo jumbo spitter
master among his slaves
jesus-obatala-sango-ogun-and-all-that-jazz
anything-to-save-me-from-this-hell
anything-to-take-me-from-this-death)

with his wand the messiah came
his herd of slaves to save and claim
over to the land of cane they came
to cultivate
to pick
to be civilized
to be picked clean

hold your head high
my brother
saved you are from family
saved from culture
saved you are from Africa
some glory glory hallelujah

my sister
saved you are from the rapist slavemaster
saved into drudgery in the master's house
saved you are into the life of a nanny for your
little massa

hold your head high
while the master and his mistress are mating in the barn
while the whip is walloping your ass
while the race is being razed into oblivion

but when oh when
my people
when will you stop licking the man's ass
when
will you reawaken and remember the pride of the past
when
will you face the facts of life
when
will you know that christianity and civilization come
together in racism
when
will you stop living lies
when
will you be
YOU
FREE
?

one view from abroad

(for a time past but present)

guns were spraying hell-fire
into innocent bodies
brothers were killing brothers

indiscriminately in the name of freedom
each side proclaimed holiness and righteousness
absolutely in the name of freedom

and we stayed out for fear of
dying
happy to be away from it all
boasting our cleanliness and happiness
knowing our happiness was a farce
our quietude a superficial nonsense
and our brothers and sisters and mothers and fathers
were being
wasted
in a war meaning nothing but
death

some became merchants of war
selling and sensationalizing notions of death disease damnation
pretending to be ambassadors of a cause no more than personal
reaping the fruit of others' desperate labour
and some were purveyors of peace
selling silence heavy with hypocrisy
saying nothing meaning much
about our still-born nation

blinded by hate born of hunger for green-backs
brothers exchanged grimaces and snares
we were blind to our fate as
victims
victims of the despicable greed of
shepherds
victims of their
self-interest
victims of our sham innocence lethargy fear and sense of survival
victims of our
guilt
today...

today
the guns are silenced they say forevermore
even while they are shooting and shouting
and we're watching and waiting for
nothing
safe in our innocence
today...

today
we forget the past
today we fear the past
for the present is the past
today.

original blackie

he's walking on air
striding haughtily down the teeming tropical street
wrapped in his made-to-measure elegant suit
his alligator shoes reflecting light
strong enough to blind an unshaded eye
his cologne stinks from here to eternity
the latest on the american market he's quick to assert
that's the original blackie for you

mr. original stops to chat
with a group of admiring underlings
with dreams of america jutting out of their heads
that's far from being the right word
for the man's giving a monologue
a spirited discourse-with-self
about the ever-popular subject
of the black african's originality
his acceptance the world over
his privileged situation
as compared with others less fortunate
especially in a paradise named america

america. america. america.
of course, he was in america for years
whenever he had problems minor problems
he simply threw on his flowing robe

his distinctly african attire
to prove his originality. uniqueness. blackness.
he also used his sing-song african talk
pronto everything was all right
the civilized folks knew his identity
for which he was proud ever so proud and
honoured!

so mr. africa never stops swelling
under the yoke of civilization
spreading his empty notions among the unknowing
the peacock among meagre hens
the fast-mouthed stooge
who does not give a damn about your heritage
his hair's all conked up and they call it process
like a mind warped by shallow thoughts shady notions process of the head of the
brain of life
his tribal marks have been messed with
in an attempt to change the past
he even speaks a language called american and he ain't jiving
the jive-turkey
like a robot
and you'll never take him for a lousy african...
dig?

mr. africa is a big big deal
black outside indescribable inside
always mesmerizing his faithful audience
many of them are already away in the promised land america. america. america.
too late will they see
through mr. snow of the tropics

Ossie Enekwe

Ossie Enekwe was born 12 November, 1942 in Affam, Enugu. He has been ably described as gifted in 'garnering shards of diverse experiences, transmuting them, and crafting them into a mould which is thoroughly humanized and constantly affecting.' Over the years, his artistic use of words to express his innermost thoughts and feelings has given birth to many works of art.

He was Vice President of the Association of Nigerian Authors (ANA), (1988-1991), and editor of many local and international journals. In fact, he was script writer on Literature for the Christian Radio Studio, Enugu, 1966-1967.

Marching to Kilimanjaro, a collection of poems to be published by Malthouse Press Limited, is his latest work. It is a collection every poet would love to read. It is inspiring and didactic.

Enekwe is Professor of Dramatic Arts and Co-ordinator of Dramatic Arts, University of Nigeria, Nsukka, Nigeria.

Solitude

(In memory of Nnabuenyi Ugonna)

Gently like travelling clouds
mankind drifts into eternity,
generation after generation,
layers of graveyards across the world.

Think of all the pieces of cloud
sailing gently to eternity
beautiful faces in a crowd,
honeyed voices in a passing encounter,
laughter and glitter
of teenage girls,
toddle of infants,
swaying dance of flowers.

See the tender feathers
of the butterfly,

heavenly colours
in the underbelly of the cobra,
orange membrane
in the robin's open mouth.

Hear the invisible breeze
fleeting silver on green grass.
Lament the pain in the guts of the poor,
homeless, bemused, afraid of entangling

Feel life in the bones of elders,
soul in rocks in the heaving mountains.
Rejoice in the beauty of creation:
voices of humanity trapped in mud,
memories of loved ones lost in the wind.
Solitude.

Raven Day

(For Major-General Mamman Vatsa, OFR)

What prayers can eclipse
this raven day of purple newsblast?
What fate hurled you
into this gully of helplessness?
Inscrutable fate hovers on its horrid wings.
Relentless time rolls forward
on armoured wheels
Death approaches with its basket
for a harvest of skulls.

But think of gun barrels as water hoses,
a hall of bullets as a shower of rain,
gun blast as the terrible voice of God
calling you to His merciful bosom.

Pardon the echoing distance
between friends lost in harmattan haze.
Pardon the misery of flowers
rushed by fetid waters.
Pardon...pardon...

Big Fish, Small Fish

                Big fish eat small fish,
                big men, small men,
                in the belly of night.

Light and dark clash in the lagoon.
Malignant weeds sit on the oblongata of the noon.,
King-sized fishes suck up the salt of the sea
Tiny ones lie prostrate for fleas.

                Big fish eat small fish,
                big men, small men,
                in the belly of night.

Contractor-leaders carouse with lovers.
Drunken giants snore in granite towers.
Hungry workers shrivelling into their pants,
scratch the dust like ants.

                Big fish eat small fish
                big men, small men,
                in the belly of night.

At the rising of the sun,
the poor escape their hovels.
At the edges of city motels,
a million fingers tear through refuse cans.

                Big fish eat small fish,
                big men, small men,
                in the belly of night.

mandatory song

Questions!
Hard facts!
Needles and pain!

Human dignity is
our mandatory song.

We grope in a dark route
with its plenitude of smoke
leaking fuel and mustard.

A burning winter!
The youth flee
the damp watts of home
roll downtown through hell
in search of fleeting contentment.

I remember Cindy
who arrived Saturday
departed Sunday
moving even onwards
in her hand a linen bag
full of memories.

She rolled along
in search of peace
gathering the world
yet travelling light.

Ekene*

(For Joe & Carol Bruchac & Family)

Ekene to this house
home of a lion, lioness
and their golden haired cubs.
Ekene dili uno-a![1]

1've passed through your threshold,
relished its lovely sounds and smells,
slumbered here in Summer and Winter.
Love to this house, palace of love!

Across seven seas I flew,
a bird of passage with a passing song,
black wings ruptured by falcons.
My songs which will not thrive on Broadway

bloom and blow with your accompaniment.
Here I set the drums of *Obunenu*,[2]
for we are one
in the glorious dust of eternity.

This is a love of many years,
purged of all brittle sentiments.
Condensed without mercy,
it sounds as lovely as a golden gong.
E*kene*, to this house!

Ekene, Igbo word for greetings
[1] Greetings to this house!
[2] *Obunenu*, music from the shrines at Affa, birthplace of the poet.

Situation Report

Poverty flows like poison
in the blood vessels of toiling people.
Fear knocks perpetually on their bones.
Dawn yields no sunshine.
The ignorant and undernourished poor
blame fate for their misery,
eulogize the flatulent rich
for little flavours.
The poor delude themselves
that they too will flourish.

Yellow feelings where injustice reigns.
Yellow life of the poor
Yellow light at dusk when drunken bones shrivel.

Over pot-holes, muddy ponds and battered pavements, through brambles, over
rivers of crocodiles
that bare their maws
at the laughing whiteness of the sky,
the lonely, abandoned wretch trudge on,
breeding and dying, eyes blurred by salty sweat,
hearts burning with inchoate rage

But, through knowledge, intellection and work,
we will give this rage the firmness and potency
of rockets and bazookas, streaking fast against
the assumed permanence of injustice.
Through love for truth and beauty,
we will create that world
where the hawk and the eagle
can perch, none displacing the other.

Harry Garuba

This poet who has an incomparable sensitivity towards man's struggle for self actu-alisation and fulfillment was born in Akure in 1958. He lived in various parts of the West and Midwest before proceeding to Government College Ughelli for his sec-ondary education.

Harry Garuba is today a lecturer in the English department of the University of Ibadan. He has many works of poetry to his credit. He edited the collection of poems by young writers, *Voices From the Fringe* published by Malthouse Press Limited.

Shadow and Dream

a band of worshippers insolently intone
incantations beneath the tattered shawl of leaves

a little bird flaps its wings in the thin air
drenched in the full colour of sunset

a leaf stirs with the light wings of a meteor
and drops silently into my childhood nest of laughter

and I recall, through frayed amber edges of a blurred past
the memory of the strange quiet of an evening

an evening in the tale of elders
I recall a dream of wings and the horizon.

Estrangement: Kano '78

(for a friend, Comrade Peasant)

Walking along craggy footpaths,
dusty, save for the lenience of the wind;
footpaths careering along a landscape
of drought, into the belly of a land
in famine

I watched

bare-footed children in ragged clothes,
white ragged clothes, (we are a
religious people), turning russet-coloured
in a silent covenant with the amber
of a waning day

I watched

shadows lengthening into the dusk,
the invasion of a gnawing silence,
shredded, occasionally, by animal sounds:

the whistle of a homing bird,
the frightened screech of an owl,
the hum of descending darkness
and

I went

passing on my way, herdsmen
returning, rod across the shoulders,
to the peasant peace of loving arms,

the pleasant filth of rotting shacks
but

I saw

the soothing pain of wounded dreams,
dreams shorn of wings, of colour,
of vice, of tone: dreams ruptured

in the rank screams of poli-trick-cians

In league

businessmen, professionals, prophets,
professors and
poets singing in the chloroform dream of money
And

I felt
I felt

estranged. Surely the poet is
estranged who cannot share
his people's fount of being.

Bubble

Watching
a little bubble
inflate itself
with the wind of a dream
rising with the longing of hope
to fly from the depth of despair
to emerge from the quicksands of anguish
to stand daintily on a little tendril of love
to explode with the seminal fluid of sea-wine

I hold in my wounded breast the perpetual pain
and its memory
and hug with blood-warmth
the secret eternal pain and dream of a bubble.

Tower of dreams

let my hand touch yours
across this mist of time.
a feel of the flesh
let my tear join yours
across this gulf of anguish:

a well of water.
I will erect your suffering
into a tower of dreams for future generations.
                    (mother and child)

As she bent camel-burdened
With dawn bubbles between her teeth
Her human load crying on her back
She bunched up her buttocks and adjusted her hips
Again tying the new load with her ancient cloth
Waiting for the sun to rise above the rain at the cloud's end.

At suncall she will be here to reap
The delight of -tears in the leaf's eye
For she has woven garlands of sorrow
On an eve that died with the wind's sigh
Among the twisted vines of unfulfilled dreams
She will be here to reap at suncall
The scar on the earth's skin, the memory
Of a wound that stirred its virgin flesh.

She will be here at sunrise a reaper of delight
Little buds of light on her breast her waist girdled
With green beads of vegetation.

Silas Obadiah

Born in 1960 in Jengre-Jos, Nigeria, Silas Obadiah has been on the staff of the English Department of the University of Maiduguri, Nigeria. He is currently doing graduate work in the Creative Writing Programme at Brown University in the USA.

Silas Obadiah has published poems and short stories in such diverse publications as *The Chelsea, The Greenfield Review, L iwuram Fajar, Obsidian II, The Literary Half-Yearly, Poetry Australia, and The SeattleReview.* He is also widely anthologized and has a poetry collec*tion, Voices of Silence*being published by Malthouse Press Ltd.

The Sacrifice

(for Castillo)

He went on being a root in the dark
Groping his way into the breast of the earth
Not that he loved sun-rays less
But that the boughs above
May stand the blows of levelling winds

He chose to remain a bat
Groping endlessly on noxious nights
Not that he loved sun-rays less
But that his peers born with tearful brows
may see their way to enviable heights

He remained mute, songless
Denying himself the lucid taste of tunes
So that the lips of his peers
Will be bouquet of pleasing songs

He was to die with his green foliage
Not that he loved the lease of life less
But that the greying leaves of his comrades
Might know the magic flavour of life

And so he remained a searching root in the dark
Groping endlessly on noxious nights,
His lips sealed from the beauty of son
And his life fleeing from the green foliage
Not that he loved sunlight less
But that his peers wrapped in endless depths
Will climb to enviable heights

The Poet's Cry

(For *Tanure)*

This was from the poet:

Will anyone tune his ears to my song
When I am only shrub among poplars?
When I am outside the row of the eminent?
When my crude horns cannot blast beyond the hills?
When my sun cannot rise from the east?
When my star has no place in the sky?
When my eagle has no branch to perch on?

Yet when he sang:

I saw the secret mysteries of the earth
I saw the shrub towering above poplars
I saw him leading the row of the eminent
I saw kings dancing to this endless songs
I saw the dead woken by his horn blast
I saw the star sparkling in the sky
I saw his sun rising from the east
I saw his eagle perching on giant *iroko trees.*

Beggars

The wind rapes their shaky sleep
And stretches their winding nights to millenniums

The trees scorn their bleeding plight
By swaying myriad arms in the sky

The rain plunder their shacks
And send them groping into doom

God hears their pleading cries
And sends manna from the sky

And the poet howls their woes
And is branded spinner of worthless yarns

And so they live, so they die
These makers of gods

These makers of poets.

Phanuel Akubueze Egejuru

Born on 21 November, 1942 in Avu-Owerri, Nigeria, Phanuel Akubueze Egejuru got her Teachers' Certificate from Women's Training College, Umuahia, and attended the Universities of Ibadan and Minnesota where she graduated with a *Magna Cum Laude* in French. She continued her studies at the University of California Los Angeles (UCLA) where she completed an MA in French and a PhD in Comparative Literature. Ten years later she returned to UCLA to complete another masters degree in Public Health, specializing in population, family and international health.

Egejuru has taught at several American universities,; including UCLA, University of California at Riverside State University of New Yolk (SUNY) at Brockport, and University of Rhode Island. She also taught at the Universities of Dar es Salaam, Tanzania and Imo State, Nigeria. She is presently teaching English at Loyola University in New Orleans, USA.

Her publications include several scholarly articles, two books of criticism, *Black Writers, White audience. A Critical Approach to African Literature (1978), and Towards African Literary Independence: A Dialogue with Contemporary African Writers (1980)*, and a novel, *The Seed Yams Have Been Eaten.*

Uluji*

Her name is tattooed on her arm.
ULUJI, whose beauty is legend,
Brown earth in a statuesque pose.
Tall, straight and graceful,
She was solid femininity.
With the unblemished hue
Of aja ozu. **
Angelic legs on shapely feet
With Nefertitian neck
That craned many necks;
All is gone to waste, consumed
by the dust..
The circular oval face,
ULUJI—gone to feast
With the ancestors.

And how your outline
Hangs in my mind,
Like mirage on a hot tarmac road,
Tempting my pen and brush.
Can I dare verbalize or paint you,
ULUJI—that which nature
Made perfect?
Where should I begin,
Head or toe?
ULUJI, your beauty
Was wrapped
In a tall phrase—
ULUJI nwanyi mara nma OKPU!***

*An elegy composed by the poet for her mother's memorial service in 1984.
**Reddish brown earth from the inner chambers of an anthill.
***ULUJI, woman of eternal beauty.

I, Woman

The riddle of my genesis is in Genesis.
I, woman, have solution to the enigma
Of my essence and my being.
I, woman, conceived in the rib cage of a deep sleep
And delivered of my father by
The first Midwife, God Himself.
I, woman, helpmate to my parent,
Play triple roles of wife, mother, daughter.
Over the years I have evolved and
So has the riddle of my genesis.
But my evolution has brought regrets
To my parent and his midwife.
I, *wo*, come before *man,* error
Corrected by the motion of years.
I, woman, can no longer claim to be the flesh of my
father's bone;
I will no longer bear the triple burden
To the man who gave birth to me.
I, woman, shall be the Creator And the Creature of Myself.

Tell me about Africaw

Sister, tell me about Africaw.
Sure! What do you want to know?
Do you guys have schools in Africaw?
No, we don't, that's why we come to learn from you.
How com yo'all speak English so good?
Try African History, it will help.
Say, Sister, do you guys still live on trees?
Yes, we do.
That's cool. How do you get up there?
With elevators of course.
Not the Tarzan way?
No, that's too primitive for us tnat is.
Say, I hear you guys buy wives.
We sell them. That's how You Guys got here.
Sister, did you ever rode on a elephant?
Yes I did, here in San Diego zoo.
Say Brother, you don't have to go to Africaw.
The jungle is right here in Americaw.

Emevwo Biakolo

Emevwo Biakolo is a lecturer in the English Department, University of Ibadan. He has been described by critics as a *wordsmith* who deftly weaves words - despiring words, comforting words, destructive words, creative words - to produce humour, wit and irony.

Among his collections are *Strides of the Night,* a collection of thought-provoking poems, and *Ravages and Solaces*, both to be published by Malthouse Press Limited in 1995.

Secrets of the Sensorium

We shall see the night's stain
Through the crystal of dawn;
And smell the virus
in the nostrils of the microscope.

We shall touch the nugget
with the hand of the hammer;
And the haysack needle
with the finger of fire

The cancer in the tickle
of the surgeon's knife;
The insult's question
in the answer of the slap

The secrets of locking limbs
in the swelling of the stomach;
The meaning of the ram's bleating
in the syntax of the blade

        and the glory foretold
        and the truth untold

But we shall behold:

The vulture in man
in the scavenging of the urchin

And hear:

The rumble of hunger
in the throat of death.

We will see:

The fullstop of famine
on the page of the riot

And know:

The innards of jails
in the carving knife of revolt

The serpent in SAP
in the cage of a probe

The heel of the tyrant
on the string of his fall

For we shall know:

The menace of the smile
in Nineteen-ninety-two!

Memories of Hidden Things

Who remembers
the ram's anguish
in the delight of mutton

The itch
in the hen's vagina
in the making of omelette

Or the cow's lowing
in the frying of veal

Who remembers
the silence in the footfall of dawn
when her saffron robe blazes
in the fire of noon

                    and the fatal visions:

Who sees
The state head
on the neck
of the Staff Chief

The night
in the womb
of the day

Or the death throes
in the sweetness of smiling mushroom. . .
                    with other palingenesis

And all that we did
And all that we are
And all we shall think
In the loins of our fathers

And the feet
of the will
entangled in the heart's plot

And the hidden wish
 In the rancour of rejection;
And the pining for Christ
In the heart of the devil

Do Not Say I Told You

Do not say I told you so
But:

When the tyrant wakes quaking
In the middle of the night
And he hears the owl's hooting
In the howls of his victims

It is the liquid of fear
in the heart of stone;
then it's time to split the service
in three secret arms

When the teacher rubs his pate
With the chalk of penury
And his loins rage for compensation
In the bed of his pupil

it is the power of the red pen
across the exercise book
it is the stomach's swelling
with the food of knowledge

And the judge's perjuries
in the muffle of his robe
And the lawyer's victory
In the purse of the jury

will be told
in the court of the marketplace

But do not say
I told you so:

For the bowels of Kirikiri
Are fathomless as hell
And who would lick
His sapped soup bowl in peace
Must learn the trapped howl
Of silence.

The End of the Cycle

We pleaded for our Kingdom
From our foes our brothers,
For our fields
And watering places;
they gave us stone countries
rocky lands in desert spaces.

We pleaded for our peace
For little loves of labour;

they gave us horsewhips
and blood-bags of war.

We counselled patience,
Made waiting our word;
they swore more scorpions
to our welted backs

And now the dimmed-tide shall burst
And we shall show murder her face
As fire drives out fire
So blood shall blood

We shall take the blood
Out to the streets
With our bowl of justice;
We shag take the blood
Out of the cloakrooms
And the tea-rooms
Out of mansions and barracks

We shall pour the blood
Of the barracks and the mansions
Out on the fields

And we shall sing
With our ploughs
To the fields
And make our peace in our places.

The Rime of an Aesthetic Poet

A loneliness ago
When our hearts rode
The nightsteeds of desire
We chanced upon
The byway of love
And on a pleasure grove
Dismounted:
our souls trod to measures
of our flesh...

The stars were bright
And our spirits right

But there was no moon
And her maiden with the wink.

The insects chirped
From the cords of our heart
Their voices making love
To the soft flesh of the wind

The smells keyed desire
To a pitch
Nor were there joys
We could not reach:
   yet when desire comes
   can regret be far behind?

For I have seen these kingdoms
And drank life to the lees

I have gathered experience
As the dung beetle gathers turd

And seen the world
As a roach in the bin

I have loved the Man
With the heart of a whore
And made my moments
In the weakness of wine

Traversing my land with
My experience and my love
I have choked on cinders
Of the remembrance

On these I have fed to the brim
With a gleam
Yet could not glimpse a dream
E'en in the dim

I have cluttered the world
With my words:
Who'd cut the cords
That they furled?

The Living and the Death
(To Okpako before his birth)

I

(To my Son)

My son, look not for yourself in you
But let your gaze wander
Far away
To the slender pines that
Whistle a plaint to the wind
To the rodents that scurry
Across the weed-platted paths
To the dark streams that ripple
Over forest trees and the tall ferns.

My son, fear the gift
of the Greeks
*(Gnothi Seuthon)
That is for old men
Wizened by gout and gin and faded dreams,
For the living-dead
Whose spirits bleed and are maimed,
For the dead who are dead
But would not die

My son, look not for yourself in you
But beyond you
And let your spirit

Know thyself;
At the lintel of the
Delphic Oracle.

Scan the giddy heights
Where truth droops golden from the bough
And seek among the wayfarers
The haven of peace
For truth dwells not in
But beyond the man.

II

(On the Departure of a Beloved)

Now that she is gone
And the light has vanished
From our skies
Let its repair to the backyard
And on the crust of earth, kneel
To sing our sorrow

The end of life's pulse
Is like the death of a song
Its echo haunts the dreams of night
And makes the livelong day
Vibrant with mystic notes
That never cease.

The memories of the dead
Are beautiful like the sheening fire
Of the dying sun on the grey hills
For then the living are
Witnesses of a heaven
That glows on the earth.

So now that she is gone
And we have shed our tears
Let us remember only this:
The dead
Are like the soul's song:
Their memory is forever.

Benin Republic

D'Almeida. Ismaili.

Irene Assiba D'Almeida

Born in Dakar, **Senegal,** where she spent most of her, childhood, Irene Assiba D'Almeida is a **citizen** of the Republic of Benin. She did her undergraduate studies at the Université **d'Amiens** in France where she obtained a Licence d'Anglais, and then went on to **the** University of Ibadan, Nigeria, where she took an MPhil degree. Her PhD is from Emory University in the USA.

Irene D'Almeida has taught at a number of universities, including the University of Kentucky. She is currently teaching French and African literature at the University of Arizona at Tucson. Her interests span literature, culture, languages, literary theory, women studies, and translation. Apart from publishing several scholarly articles of criticism, Irene D'Almeida co-translated Chinua Achebe's *Arrow of God* into French. Her articles have appeared in *Presence Africaine, Ufahamu, Meta: Journal des Traducteurs,* and *Theory Into Practice.* Her poems are featured in an anthology edited by Carole Boyce Davies titled, *Black Women's Writing: Crossing the Boundaries.*

Quicksand

Playfully you took my hand
I felt free
To run with you
In the fields
Of red sand
And did not see
The rich red earth
Turn into deadly dunes
Beyond the desert

Now
My feet once so resolute and firm
Have fallen out of step

Defenceless
In my leap to your land
In your lethal quicksand
I can only sink
                    sink
                    sink

Playfully you took my hand
I felt free
To run with you
In the fields
Of red sand
And did not see
The rich red earth
Turn into deadly dunes
Beyond the desert

Why Yallah takes

Yallah, the Great Eye,
Was watching over Ani,
His favourite daughter.
Crafty in creative play,
Ani, the Earth, moulded out of clay
Perfectly cast little men and women.
Yallah celebrated in their beauty.
Gently, gently,
He blew Breath into them
And the clay images came sparkling with life.
Soon these men and women tilled the land
With a loving, loving hand.
And Ani blossomed with delight
Yallah, the Great Eye,
Saw Ani's prosperous swell.
Nobody knew
If it was from surprise
Or jealousy.
But to his Palace, he called Ani
And half of her children he demanded.
Ani wilfully pleaded·
Everything belonged to Him, she knew;
But from her loved ones, she could not part.
Yallah demanded again and again.

But still Ani pleaded.
Yallah suddenly ballooned,
Swelled in rage;
Ordained that Ani's loved ones
Be forever locked in her womb.
And each time Yallah recalls
How Ani went astray,
He takes a breath of life away.

Rashidah Ismaili

Born in the Republic of Benin of a Beninoise mother and Nigerian father, Rashidah Ismaili was educated in Benin, France, Italy and the USA. She was married to a Nigerian and now lives with her adult son in Harlem, New York, where she runs Salon d'Afrique.

Rashidah Ismaili is a lecturer in Africana Literature and Black Psychology at Rutgers University in Newark, New York. She also serves as the Assistant Director of HEOP, an academic support programme for minority students.

Active in numerous cultural organizations and a founding member of Calabashe Poets, she lectures both nationally and internationally at such universities as the University of Hawaii and Universidad International of Puerto Rico. Her manuscript of vignettes titled, *Tableaux d'Afrique,* has just been published.

Letters-11

Dear Friend,
You are the
pregnant pause of peace
that breaks the silence
of winter without flowers.

Your smile is the gift
of sunshines when summer
is a far off dream and
winter whitens my
landscape. The intimacy
of hearts strong enough to
share past secrets and
brave enough to bare
our bosoms to the cold
impersonal stares of
those whose lives
harbour unfocused anger.

We must needs pronounce
kindness for each other
and best wishes to them
who are needful but
too weak to say...
'Hello.'

Forgetful

Each day
they get up tired and silent.
Each day
they pull on
dirty pants.
Each day
they rise
tired and weary.
Each day
they drink
a single cup'o.
Each day
they chew
a yesterday's biscuit.
Each day
they go out
in chilly morning air.

And
they go down
down, the road.
And
they go down
down the long road.
And
then they wait
and wait on the road.

And
then they wait
and look,
wait and look.
And
then down,

down, down, the road,
down the road a truck comes.
Each day
they wait
as they did the day before.
Each day
the truck comes down
down the road.
Each day
the men pile
dark and tight.
Each day
they over-crowd
the truck that comes.
Each day
they wait
and go with the truck

And
the truck
is dust-dark and big.
And
the truck goes down
down, down, down a long road.

And
the truck heads
straight for the border.

And
they go
the men who work.
The tired men
go down,
down in the ground.
And
they see sun slide
as they go down.
And
it is dark
when they come up.
Each day
they move
not think
move,

One foot,
then
the other.
And
on
and
on
and
on...

Cameroun

Kombem. D'Almeida.

Sim Emmanuel-Ngwainmbi Kombem

Born in 1962 in Belo-Kom, Cameroon, Sim Kombem attended the Government Primary School, Bali; St. Bede's College, Ashing-Kom; CCAST, Bambili, and eventually, took the BA in English and Literature from the University of Yaounde, also in Cameroon. He obtained an MA from Jackson State University and a PhD in Mass Communications at Howard University, all in the USA. He teaches at Florida Memorial College and St.Thomas, University.

Kombem's writings appear in several publications, including *New Directions, The Mould, New Horizons, Janus, The Continent, Cameroon Tribune,* and *Cameroon Outlook.* He has published two books of poetry, *Sims Poetic Column* and *A Bush of Voices,* and a novel, *Dawn in rage.*

Jinkfuin* at Dawn

here come ceaseless dew drops sinking on all
from the sky
bringing to you a land all white and new

see what the birds do
they take their flight by the hill
look at the cottony clouds settling on him
by morning light he will soon grow grey
and all Jinkfuin will come out to say
the gods of peace are early today

on the long grass roofs
sweet smelling wisps of smoke feed the air
within the scattered mounds of huts
folk cook and eat
when dawn is gone
folk would come
sprinting along muddy footpaths
       raffia palm baskets girded on their

strong diligent backs
farm bound to harvest corn for evening meal

Jinkfuin, a hamlet in Kom, place of *Afo-A-Kom deity, located in the Northwest province in Cameroon.*

Letter to Pastor

They sit like drovers saying evening prayers
They dip their heads as ducks do
and lift their heads as ducks do

Soon two cheap skirts
with
bags of books hung across their fallen breasts trudge in
                    One would think they thirst
But they giggle and giggle
                    as the day of promotion exams dawns

They hide about in swamps in search of some serene secret seed
                    embalmed in tufts of flesh
They raise their heads high in search of suicide

        Pastor
                    Do they destroy Cupid's law
                    Do they

The vicar scolded me
and returned to his bible

Another Moment

                I
            stand alone
        eager to hate the guts
you used in wooing a virgin who longed for
the chalk of civilization scratched all over her.
Your little poems, false ramblings
In gin bottles.
Your strange feelings for her, those framed words
of yours faked as affection that have destroyed older girls,
haunt her now like a benign rabbit on a hot summer noon,

panting under stale breath; her little eyes burning;
her fresh bosom sizzling under your large body;
her mind dancing, fiddling to discover you;
her nude self coiling and closing before you
kill me slowly like AIDS.
If i die
I will weather countless thunderstorms
and lightnings, sufficient to burn your thicket.
But if i have wronged the world
If i have spelled love upside down,
If i have dug trenches for escape duikers, or
for lost lambs fleeing from the flames of wild
bush fires
O please forgive,
you little lambs leaning up on sleeping lions,
basking under summer sun with leopards.
With cold ashes of love shaking from a gentle breeze, single
do
i
stand
eager to pound my name,
to watch the silhouettes of an early affection pine out
beneath my steady gaze
to read my revelries before they fade behind twilight clouds,
to hatch my egg-dreams before they crack.

Stopping by a poultry

                    Here
is the fowls parliament which stretches out into the horizon
And here
                    Aban
shambles in with a can and makes a stand
Up
the parliamentarians rise and chirp and cluck
their red necklaces dangle
their shirts shimmer
Up
they rise
their white socks dipped in straw
their eyes tottering on Aban while the others perch to,
hatch

See their chipped mouths between the bamboo window clucking

the midday air
I think they are thirsty

Aban plods on and on
leaving water can in each stall and caressing their red shirts

The harmattan flows in and the fowls are quiet for a moment

Fernando D'Almeida

Born on 19 April, 1955 in Douala, Cameroon, Fernando D'Almeida is a journalist, literary critic, and speaker, who works for the national newspaper,*Cameroon Tribune*. He has published four books of poetry:*Au Seuil de l'exile, Traduit du je pluriel, En attendant le verdit,* and, *Lespace de la parole.*

By Forty-Sixth

So many times
I walked and walked
Following orders
But all is futile
I approached the man
Who loiters along the quay
In search of real life
I was not to blame
If to blame is to be lost
In the network of insignificant things
I played the game to discover myself
I told my childhood love
I drank to the health of life
I laughed at my reassuring ignorance

I looked into things
Things were revealed to me
While I reconciled my life
With the life of others
I didn't hide my face
In swaddling clothes of infamy
I passionately uttered an equivocal yes

I am aware of my crazy life
I have reasons for my madness
I didn't reach out to others

Except to be human myself
I am standing firm
As I keep my stand
I shall not let myself be battered by doubt.
I am as secured as Fire

The path of shattered hopes

of course nobody is forced
to guarantee my fantasies
to go back with me on the path
of shattered hopes
that I take each day
to reach the borders of my dreamland

I know I must invent
another outcry more conformed to reality
to avoid being trapped by the day
whose vocation is to make us
take risks when
all seems to be at stake

but how difficult it is
to echo sometimes what others say
to demand a place in the sun for yourself
without being forced to be submissive
and to kneel before the old people
to be a sycophant of dictators

do I have to think about life
so full of frustrations
will useless combats ever be sufficient
to snatch me from everyday confusion
if only I would be able to know
what tomorrow might be
would I not go to dance *makossa* on the moon

it is up to Fate to decide if I should
continue to journey in my insanity
or if I must stop being far from reality
and put my feet again in the muddy clay
instead of walking on the paths of sand and gravel
that lead to home on the local road

it is Destiny who reiterates inattentively
confidence in mankind
our prejudice against a person going his own way
like a cadaver groaning for life
and his last recommendations
to Destiny of curse against the arbiter

Equatorial Guinea

Udofia

Carlos Udofia

Born on 27 July, 1962 in San Carlos, Equatorial Guinea, Carlos Udofia virtually grew up in Nigeria. He had both his primary and secondary education in Obotim Nsit and Mbioto II, both in Akwa Ibom State of Nigeria. Between 1981 and 1985 he studied Town and Country Planning at the Polytechnic, Calabar, in the neighbouring Cross-River State.

Carlos Udofia has many works of poetry among which is *Amen.* In 1986, he was awarded a National Honours Award in the Nigerian National Youth Service Corps.

But how does it feel?

But how does it feel
To be the donkey? To be the quarry?

But how does it feel when the scrotal stones
Of manhood are smashed between stones
When the innocent toes of the pullet
Are crushed on stones
When the crow on the tree-top
Out-dirges the mutilated ones ... ?

How does it feel to be chained:
Sentried over the giggles and chuckles.
THEY MAKE LOVE TO OUR WIVES...

And, how does it really feel
To watch from without the cordon
The endless trips of the sumptuous spoons
Shovelling up and munching down

—The sheer peace of minds?

Taken. And robbed brazen.
In the cold
          In the bitter cold.

And he tried to grasp the thin air
But everything slipped away.

Taken. Stripped and broken.
 In the cold

          In the bitter cold.

When the night is darkest
And the elements most savage.

Who was here—
The Truncheon of law:
          The armour and the shield!

ONCE AGAIN master will come to table
Connect the cables
& give every panther his cigar:
Watch the mean darts of the crumb-gatherers!
You cannot forget your duty:
Chain the world under
When master's having His Peace of Mind!

Oh, what souls are moved by these
Mother, Africa: on death throes,
Turning in the critical hour...
On every path on every creek
Withering stalks, tortured breaths, knit
Desperate pleas to deaf gods

Ensconced on iron, on wooden thrones...
Your woes yield dividends enough
For their weal who savage rods rule
The unmoaned night of your days...

Where is born to us
The deliverer maker of dreams?

You cannot know

SHE KNEELS THRO HER PRAYERS.
The burden of her sighs
The helplessness of her tears
All jewelled with bitter but good-natured smile
—Set like a moon in a crown of thorns:
Delicate upon the table!

HIS MIND FEEDS ON SILENCE, and she dies
Piecemeal awaiting the answers.

You cannot know
Yon walked in from the rain;
Wrecked youth of a troubled age,
That no...or what sadness
What wound what alarm •
Can stir again the frozen embers

Of the chequered brotherhood?
The fires went out long long ago

And the hearth is cold—
As his mind
Which feeds on, which moves;
If it must at all, grimly
In utter silence.
So, if she dies piecemeal

Awaiting the answers,
Though you pray and tell on rosaries
Your mouthful of hopes must turn to ashes.
Ah! how many times
Have you turned in your numbed cheeks
The cold ashes of how many hopes—

Standing there
Unable to swallow, unable to spit out?

Though the pendulum of your mind strikes:
Go? knock! go! knock! go! knock! blow!!!

You cannot know
That you mustn't break down or cry
That you mustn't set the house on fire
That the loaded head of the house
Is having
          HIS PEACE OF MIND!
Pass out with me in silence
Lest, to spite a face, we wreck our heritage
Let's find some quiet spot
And there rest our chins upon our red fists.
Ah! let's go! let's go!

There must be some wisdom
We can glean
When our foreheads sweat upon
The invocations of our tapping toes.

I turn to you

I wake to dawn upon
An uncertain edge
And hold out my palms
Under the fluorescent lamp
—Stained with blood of mosquitoes:

Swarm of nuisances in season,
I cannot explain my sudden disquietude:

Am I a murderer?
I turn to you who sleep here
Naked beside my breast—
So profound this silence our pulses
Beat in rhythm with the cosmic hum,

And within your sleep;
Careless, abandoned: breathes
That innocence and trust that disturb
And within it too, this sleep of yours, a snake.
The former disarms my possessive animal

The latter bestirs my curiosity
For I find in the rhythm a flower
And a dish—one to behold
The other to devour

But the sacred thread: this snake that is,

Electric between us, compelling
And inducing this overpowering
Intimacy, yet exciting
No urge for possession but rather,
In its wake, this cognition

And identification with all life,
That suddenly, all so suddenly
induces a shock that induces arrest
At mere routine of mosquito killing...
How do you explain O heart of mine?

For, to think that this blood
Here in ray palms,
Could, indeed, be mine...confounds.
My values, questions my ethics;
And my innocence is terribly scandalized.

Blushes

& WHEN I THINK ABOUT MY
                              immodesties

WHEN I THINK ABOUT MY
                              indiscretions...
I feel ... I feel ... and I am deeply humbled.
& FOR ALL THESE I CLAP FOR MYSELF.

Bah! The cruel burning blush
Of the unobserved moment

I have been a damned fool!
Walked bare arse when most I was wise!

...but who has not been a fool?

The Gambia

Sallah. Jallow

Tijan M. Sallah

Born in Serre Kunda, Gambia, on 6 March, 1958, Tijan Sallah is the editor of this anthology.

Love

I have often loved you
With the sweet grace of a giraffe
My heart's room gathers warmth
From your firewood-presence.
You have often been my pillar,
Erect stem to lean my trust.
You have often been my *bentenki tree,*
And 1, the elephant, leaning On your back.

But now it seems
You feed on my blemishes.
You see, love needs a new skin,
A new talk. Otherwise, love finds
Comfort in petty faults.

You stand now under the sun;
Your eyes collect nightmares
From the sight of me.
You grin the mixed smile
Of a hyena. You smile

When you mean the opposite.
You laugh, when you mean
A spear should be thrust
In to my heart.

But you still remind me
Of those days in *Brikama**

When you were a young girl
With some dandruff in your hair.
Those days when you were you,
Not some magazine photo model;
When success has not carved
A musky pride in your head.

You see, it seems
Time trims the genuine Out of love
If the two bean-lobes
Of love
Are not careful.
You stand there, sullen
As the sky before a rain.
Root of my heart, I want you
To rain happiness
And drift to that old earth
Where the old self dwells
In the naked love of giraffes.

I want you to wear those waist beads
And move with the tender waist-shake
Of a *laubeh.** * I want you to come,
Perfuming the air with *gonga.* ***

For I do not care
How much money you make now,
Or the type of prestige-car you drive;
Our love has never been
About benzs and jaguars.
I do not care about
How many cities you travel to,
Or men you put in their place;
Our love has never been
About your success against mine.

All I know is that

Our love has been about love,
The sweet earth-goodness love
Of tubers. And about
Our children and
The seeds they should gather
To plant trees of the future.

And if things should intervene,
They should only be treated as things.
And love should still be love,
And make-ups still makeups,
Before we lose ourselves
In this mad harvest of city lights.

*Brikama is a Gambian town about 26km from the capital city of Banjul; **Laubeh is a member of the lower caste of the Fulani ethnic group found in Senegal and Gambia. They are reputed for their seductiveness and sexual prowess. ***Gongais a powdery incense worn around the waist by Senegambian women as deodorant.

Radiance of a new beginning
(for Christopher Okigbo)

Birds empty their dreams under the moon's taillight.
The elephants must go; the birds gather to celebrate
Their fate.
The elephants have trampled on too many saplings.

The elephants must go.
The elephants must go.

In the summer of our laughter,
Between the whiff of corn tassels,
The elephants stole our harvests of freedom,
Banked them in their puff and pomp.

They tossed beaks into their prison saucepans.
They toasted bird-urine as wine in their triumph
They feasted on bird-meat with unrelieved glee.

The elephants must go.
They have feasted on too much vanity.
The elephants must go

With their praise-singers and gong.
They have hawked the land
Of its most precious chicken.
They have preyed on every syllable,
Abolished words and enslaved them
to their liking.

The elephants must go.
We have no need for their muscles.
In Bamako, the birds have risen—
They celebrate with binges and calabashes of *kous-kous*.
Concerts of laughter parade the streets.
An elephant has fallen.
More elephants must go.

The elephants must go.
They have no wisdom to offer.
Their minds are dark spaces of lucre.
Their eyes are long nights devoid of candles.
Their hearts are glowing coals of dappled bush.
The elephants must go.
They can no longer crouch under cover of promise.

Birds explode rainbow dreams in flutters of festive colours
They dust fear with their feet;
Flutter wings in their orchestra of ascension.

The birds pull the thread
Into the rainbow corners of the evening.
They stitch and stitch the suppressed promise of heaven.
Beak and claws go to work
To weave the radiance of a new beginning.

The elephants must go.
We have no need for trunks and weight.
They have trampled on seed.
They have eaten too much leaves.

Birds pull the thread
Over the undulating heights of the Kilimanjaro.
An elephant has fallen.
Kampala breathes a green lease of life.
An elephant has fallen.
Monrovia searches for its self.
An elephant has fallen.

An elephant has fallen;
More elephants must go.

In the spring of our despair,
Hope has climbed the intensity of feathers.
The elephants must go.
Birds flute a new anthem.

There is hope in the baobabs.
There is hope in the anthills.
The elephants cannot hide.
More elephants must go.

The land comes to consciousness

The land comes to consciousness,
Its freckled landscape and muddy water.
Its rolling hills gently seated
In silent communication
With the season-weary sky.
The sun howls by day
In the silence of its heat.
Listen to the wind-beaten traveller;
His face wrinkled as
The buttocks of old women.
Look at his feet, sore
From years of abandoning the land.
He trudges Western roads
In search of cowries.
Though his head is loaded
With the flicker of traffic lights
And his heart is segmented
Between Africa and Europe,
No violets grow in his hands.
The land comes to consciousness.
We must not be like the blue-eyed traveller
Running in and out of nowhere,
        Forever doped in the excitement of self,
        Forever adjusting to the fickleness of place.
We must follow rainbow signs
That lead us back to ourselves,

Back to being one with the land.

We must take advice from the rainbird.
Listen to its gospel coming
From the scarcity of seeds
In her deserted stomach.
It is the hour of warning.
When the land comes to consciousness,
It is no longer the clocks of loitering.
It is the cockcrow of homecoming-
Birds drifting back to their nests.
Fathers returning to parent
What they begot in the farmhouses.
And clumsy children, await
Like thorns, to hang on their overcoats.

Before the breaking of the fast

The disquiet in waking up, heaven subsiding.
Grace suddenly abandoned. Desires awaken
To the temptations of the sun.
The dreams the night before, carve out
In my conscience, transported me
Through the radiance of beauty, showed me
The reigns and raptures of Timbuktu.
Mansa Kankang Musa, Sunni Ali,
The weight of a past rich as embroidery.

The revelations on the pillow, a heaven
Squinting through our shortness of memory
And exaggeration of vision.
Exquisite empires, kingdoms of gold,
Iron and bronze. The goldsmiths' hands.
The blacksmiths' patience, the glow
Of fire and dust.

Time leaves no scrolls for memory;
The wand of the future marches
To cover expired heavens.

Griots should rise, pluck
The fiery strings, evoke the roots,
And leave us with memory-scrolls.

For who should forget,
Empires, rare as mermaids,
Profuse with Grace?

Griots should rise,
With batik-cloth worn as mantle,
And a voice fresher than honey.

Our branches, civilized comforts,
Are only desolate cages.
We need a calabash of dreams
To feed us into the Green Age.
O gods, the disquiet in waking up,
And be engulfed in redemptive memory.
Hunger biting my entrails,
But absorbed in meditative thirst.
My mind soars backward to Kingdoms-of-Grace
Before the Breaking of the Fast.

The Evaded Moon

Thus it seems, America is a promise, a star,
Twinkling lights locked with the
Multifarious lights of the world.
And it seems, it fathoms its heart on
An archaic swindling of feathers
From the peacock head of Chief Big Eagle.

Every season, my host-family invites me
For the Feast of Thankfulness.
And generations would come, near and far,
By wheel or wing,
And perform the rites of the pilgrims
Before television-baseball
And clinical hum of computers.

And it seems as if history is re-enacted
Around the cherrywood table.
And I am suddenly the exotic mine
For anthropological excavations:
Questions sequentially bubbling
Like single-intent pickaxes.

And it seems Africa feeds into
The untutored spaces of the American mind.
It is jungle lions and cubs;
Elephants uprooting trees
Amidst long-legged Masai-tribesmen;
Or gazelle running randomly and valiantly
On the thorn-matted safari landscape.

And it seems Africa is never
Ancient Egypt, or Benin;
Timbuktu, or Kilwa.
It seems Africa is perpetually
Cheap staple for the touristic media
A giant languishing behind the curtain,
Censored only to the famine and ruin.

And it seems America is a stage,
A landscape of clashing lights,
Populated by lovers of fiction.
Information overload leading to
Secondary grabbing of unfiltered half-truths.

And it seems Africa wallows in neglect
Like America's own feather-natives.
Or like Africa's diaspora-seeds trapped
In wolfish nets like the proverbial lamb.

And it seems to me that the
Feast of Thankfulness should
Be time to rethink the promise
Remove the cobwebs in parochial minds
Approach the Truth of the evaded moon.

Hassan A. Jallow

Born on 28 August, 1956 in Serre Kunda, Gambia, Hassan Jallow attended St. Theresa's Primary School in Kanifing and St. Augustine's High School, both in Gambia. He obtained an Associate Degree in Legal Assistance from Elizabeth Seton College, Yonkers, New York and took the BSc degree in Business Management at Mercy College, also in New York. He is currently pursuing graduate studies in the USA.

New York

A kaleidoscope of fragments,
Stone melting on iron,
Blood on steel.
Sweat and cranes
Criss-crossing dormant rivers.

Rivers
 Morbid with carcass of fish.
A dirge
To the progress
Of almighty Metal.

New York
A. cacophony of trombones,
The ghost of Anta Diop,
Einstein, Suzuki, Mahfouz

Mid-Manhattan,
Tall as Twin Towers.
A riot of lights Blazing its path.

Tragic Bed-sty, South Bronx,
All on bent knees
Pushing to escape
The shadows of plantations.

Ghana

**Anyidoho. Busia. Opoku. Agyemang.
Laing. Okai. Acquah. Odamtten**

Kofi Anyidoho

Bom in Wheta, Ghana, in 1947, Kofi Anyidoho trained as a teacher and taught Ewe and English in secondary schools before earning the BA in English and Linguistics at the University of Ghana. He did some postgraduate work at Indiana University at Bloomington, taking a PhD in Comparative Literature at the University of Texas at Austin, in the USA.

Kofi Anyidoho has taught at Cornell University, Ithaca, New York and is presently a staff of the University of Ghana at Legon.

He has published three books of poetry: *Elegy for the Revolution, A Harvest of Our Dreams,* and *Earthchild with Brain Surgery.* In addition to publishing several creative and critical works in such journals as *Okike, The Greenfield Review, and West Africa, Kofi* Anyidoho is co-editor of the 1988 BBC prize-winning poems, *The Fate of Vultures.* He has won other literary awards, including the Davidson Nicol Prize for Verse and the Langston Hughes Prize in Ghana.

Bayonets

BEFORE the season of the Bayonet
    there was the season of the Hoe,
    a season of the soul's harvest:
    We grew wonder-eyed standing
    humbled before the miracle
    of the giant Oak locked deep
    down within the tiniest mystery seed

    In those seasons of our soul's harvest
    there were such fires in our eyes.
    Our spirits flowered and petalled
    into hues of faintest rainbows,
    offering new and newer images
    of dreams we could with ten fingers
    mould into things and thoughts and hopes.

THEN they came with bulldozers.
And then the armoured cars dressed in camouflage.

NOW we plant grenades in backyard farms
Harvesting coffins
in showers of bullets and firepower.

They pick our flesh on Bayonets.

Across cold muzzles of guns
They break our sleep in two
Give one half to cannonblast

Toss one half into silence deeper
Than Volcano's bleeding core.

There will be showers at SunRise
And storms at SunDown.
Bones shall sprout tendrils more verdant
Than loveliest Green Mamba
Rivulets of venom shall water our fields
Restoring this soil to ancestral Fertile Time.

A Harvest of Our Dreams

There is a ghost
on guard
at Memory's door

scaring away those pampered hopes
these spoiled children of our festive days

The honey bee had plans in store
for his Mother-Queen: he went across the world
gathering fragrance from dreamy waterlilies
from lonely desert blooms
Some other gatherer came with plans
all for his own desires
Our hive went up in flames. I was away.

We will hum a dirge for a burden of these
winds

Memories of our honeycomb floating
through
seedtime within the soul beyond the reach of

Song
Rowdy echoes burst upon our soul's siesta

And harvests go ungathered in our time

There will be strange voices filling spaces
in our mind, weaving murmurings upon
the-broken tails of songs abandoned once in playing fields
Rumblings from our past are planting stakes
across our new rainbows
and in seasons of harvest dance
there still will be a ghost
on guard
at Memory's door

It was for shame the turtle
hid his pain beneath his shell
and crawled upon the pleasures of the sea.
His secret pain became a hidden rottenness
a poison to his smiles

We will hum a dirge for a burden of these
winds

Memories of our honeycomb floating
through
seedtime within the soul beyond the reach of
Song
Rowdy echoes burst upon our soul's siesta

And harvests go ungathered in our time
So these echoes come in ritual dance
from old homesteads where once she often sang
singing the dirge keeping the wake at endless funerals

Ootsa of the sea. I am Ootsa of the sea
I did not know it would be like this for me:
Yevu's net has caught me with my dreams.
And now we tread byways
searching passing faces for fleeting image after image
seeking kindred minds
for lost passwords into fiestas of the soul

Somehow we know the carnival days
cannot be gone so soon
We may gather again those

unfinished harvests of our soul.
Uncle Demanya shall come back home
with the bread basket of which
he sang through life across the hunger of our graves
Uncle Demanya shall come back
with the bread basket of which
he sang through life across the hunger of our graves.

Elegy for Revolution

a feverish psyche gropes for an
eye in the shrines of Xebieso
the armoured hope lies exposed
to wrath of thunderbolts

> These feet have kissed the sands of many shores
> Today they lay in cramps, crushed by revolving wheels
>   of State
> This heart has felt the warmth of love, throbbed to
> beats of a thousand joys let loose upon a festive world
> Today it is a husk of corn blown before the burning grass

The Revolution violates devotee. Beware
Beware the wrath of thunderbolts
The agonized thoughts of a detainee translate
our new blunders into nightmares of blood & sweat:
>   whips slashing through tender skins, broken bones
>   collapsing to floors of cells, tortured moans
>   bursting through concrete walls
>   tearing through clouds and skies
>   They seek refuge in house of storms
>   and a sad conscience clears a path
>   for poison arrows of gods of wrath

From sheltered yards of our righteousness
we watched the loading of an atom bomb
with a doubt on our lips, our cheeks
still blown with mirth of nights of revelry
our drunken ease forgetful of speed of light and sound:
>   The muzzled heat of Hiroshima bursts into
>   sudden flames, burns our laughter into
>   screams of blood, groping for memories of
>   feasts of flowing down turbulent gulfs

half-filled with discarded blue-prints for
a revolution gone astray into
arms of dream merchants.

Nostalgia

Above all I shall forever lament
the wisdom of those many many friends
who disinherited their souls
and chose the misery of alien joys

trapped in circles among snowfields
their spirits freeze and thaw and frost
with constant fickleness of northern winds

Once too often
they converge in smoky partyrooms
drinking hard to prove
a point only they can see can feel
arguing endless justifications
for a choice blindly made.

Between their dreams of fame
and hopes of instant wealth

the nostalgic self moans its way
through midnight storms
into dawn nightmares

reaching into distances silences...

Memories alone are not enough soulguide
into a future filled with absences.

Abena Busia

Born in Accra, Ghana, Abena Busia, spent her early childhood in Holland and Mexico before her family settled in Oxford, England. She took the BA degree in English/Literature at St. Anne's College, and the DPhil in Social Anthropology (Race Relations) at St. Anthony's College, both in the University of Oxford. Abena Busia has taught in several institutions and universities, including Ruskin College, Oxford, and Yale University. She also held post-doctoral fellowships at Bryn Mawr College and the University of California, Los Angeles. She is presently an Associate Professor in the English Department of Rutgers University.

Apart from publishing critical articles and poems in several journals and magazines, Abena Busia is widely anthologize, some of poems featured in *Summer Fires, New Poetry from Africa, MandelaAmandla,* and *Mother Tongues: A Book of African Women Poets.* Her first book of poem*s, Testimonies of Exile,* has just been published.

She views the experience of being raised in exile, an experience in her own words that is 'at once exciting and potentially alienating,' as a haunting influence in her poetic imagination. She sees her family as being spiritually united, despite the changes in her 'nomadic' childhood. She considers her poems as expressing 'this dual impulse of the otherwise ordinary drama of the shared experiences of everyday life, played out against the uncertainties of exile.'

Cold Harbour Seasons

i. Outside Autumn

I never saw your homes.

Didn't know where you vanished to
when the day was done
leaving me
to turn out lights
and lock doors.
Until now I had no voice to tell

how your nine to five friendliness
left me lonely nights.

ii.   Still Life in Winter Brown-Out

In the background
surrounding a dim-lit high-roofed hallway
dark wood panelled walls
a brown and tan checkered floor

in the middle distance
flanked by old oak banisters
a staircase, very wide
sweeping into the invisible darkness

in the foreground
dwarfed by her surroundings
and trying to turn outward
a black woman

in a brown and tan checkered coat
bracing the chill and hearing
the slam of the dark solid door
clamming behind her in the echoing silence

iii.   Summer's Poisoning ivy

Even in the sunshine
it's hard
            to disguise
the desolation
of this leaguered city.
More than its share
of solitary misery
on crazy walks in crowded streets.
A creeping lunacy blights
an ivory haven of walls towering
corridors of lost faith.

Exiles

Funerals are important,
away from home we cannot lay
our dead to rest,

for we alone have given them
        no fitting burial.

Self-conscious of our absence,
brooding over distances in western lands
we must rehearse,
the planned performance of our rites
        till we return

And meanwhile through the years,
our unburied dead eat us,
follow behind through bedroom doors.

Annotations

This last work has evidently been
many years of life in the making.
It begins with her passionate outbursts

The next section seems to be written
in bitterness some years later.
We can read the rage of love betrayed

Later, in quite muddled spurts,
s if attempting another story--
we find hope of love renewed

It's hard to fathom what came next
but clearly some years went by,
before the pencilled notes on life reclaimed

Something shattering happened.

We can't reassemble the fragments.

Illicit Passion

All our dreams are possible,
that is the danger.
the desert yields
to an impossible bloom:

a devouring magical beauty
straining for rain through a sacred earth
hiding traces of abandoned lives.

Mawu of the Waters

I am Mawu of the Waters.
With mountains as my footstool
and stars in my curls
I reach down to reap the water with my fingers
and look! I cup lakes in my palms.
I fling oceans around me like a shawl
and I am transformed
into a waterfall,
Springs flow through me
and spill rivers at my feet
as fresh stream surge
to make seas.

Freedom Rides Quiz

Can you tell me where is Dien Bien Phu?
I'll give you a clue;
Kent State is the place ride roughshod through

How d'you reach D. C. on the Freedom Trail?
It's quite a tale,
You boycott Montgomery, pass through Birmingham jail

Can you tell me what took place in Sharpeville?
I'll tell you who will;
Ask the children of Soweto if the answer rhymes with still.

The histories of nations
are in the end spelt out
only through the dying breaths

And of those now struggling to be reborn,
the first of these generations must weep
and bear a heavy burden
from age to hopeless age

on age that the children's children's
embittered children
may at the last first learn
to laugh, among the ripening fruits
they with silent tears now sow

And the next of these generations must weep again
when the first fruits die.

Kwadwo Opoku-Agyemang

Born in Ghana, Kwadwo Opoku-Agyemang is on the staff of the Department of English, the University of Cape Coast, in Ghana. He was a Fulbright Scholar-in-Residence at Clark-Atlanta University from 1988-1990. He has completed a book of poems, *Cape Coast Castle.*

Introit

AND THE sea cackled, foaming at the mouth
Till dry cracks ploughed the waves back;
Hope, said the sea, is not a method
There are too many sad stories
Carved in indifferent stones:

There is always another story
After this one is told
And words after the words
Of this world:
Did our elders not say
The boats leave but the people stay?

Behind the dawn stand
Queues of days, nibbles at debts
The lonely poor dropping from sight

Behind the dawn, nothing
Save the bones of sad stories:
History does not repeat itself
It merely quotes us
When we have not been too wise

Drumspeak

(for Nana)

HER SMILE rhymed with drums, Ama Afi

The one who got away living for Saturday, God dey:
At ninety she did what she could with her fading sight
She saw the sun go down on her children
Yaw Dankwa choked on the sad songs his trumpet made Kwame Nkroma slept
with his gun under his pillow
Then one night pulled the trigger in his sleep
Amoako went to bury the dead and never returned
And Ama Afi wondered
When her body would find the clemency of dust

Toward the end she walked far from her noon
Each morning she rose pure in the mouth of God
Then indifferent to her fate
Destroyed the silence by breaking into smiles

Looking for the river
She found the god it became
She paddled her innocence across the mute water
She prayed for those who died of too much, just too much
For those who suffered the indignity of watery death
And for those in whom life twists about like a dagger.
She reached across the rage, the habit of shrill blood
And made peace with innocence and nakedness
From desperation she carved the will to wait out every wish

Out of habit and out of life
She withheld nothing of herself
Planted herself womb and water
Where the seasons from deep antics within

And sometimes like the seasons
She wearied and returned
All is not lost yet, she'd say
And squeeze her eyes against the pain
Knees bent, she lingered into light like the dawn
Lit a pipe that the drums within may speak

Memory magnified her loss, taunted her breasts
But self-same memory turned the soil of her mind
And earth as earth never lost interest in her lot
Never forgot the dry peeling skin as answer
To the harmattan's wry challenge

She led us down the paths older than history
Through forest gloomy with growth
Lusting for sun, for the blood of saws
We surged forward avoiding water
New births falling rush-ripe all about us
In forests rough-tucked by rain

She lighted the fire and put the bowl to boil
Food for her sons, food for the years yet to come
And the smoke rose to the skies like a howl
Food for her warrior daughters
And for the unfinished ways of war

King Tut in America

(To Cheikh An ta Diop)

THEY MADE the good king pass
They bleached his skin
Cooked his hair
And turned his lips
But after 3000 years
Who could turn his head?

In the night when no one was looking
They turned off the lights
Lifted his face
Fixed his nose
Cut his name in pieces
And sealed his lips
They then charged the experts
To invent a new source for the Nile
Still they could not turn his head

I swear, I too saw King Tut
And even in profile
And beneath all that make-up
He was still smiling

After 3000 years he has not paled
So why should we?

First Trip to Sunshine

I CAME here armed to the teeth with smiles
1, Kwadwo Okoto, Suppliant, Monday-born
Son of Oboade, maker of every warming sign
Ah! Odonkoma, architect of all human soul
You have not heard me yet
I am just warming my mouth
It is said that the farthest a man can go
Is to come back home: labourer, mimic, hero
Here I am, eager for peace this tethered Thursday
And they tell me I am the silenced majority
Monday, Suppliance; Thursday, call for war
Friday, let all the wanderers come home
For, Sunday, and it is all over

Okoto, Preko, Akyin and Tanoba called Atakora·
The seed is hard; heaven has receded
Our God and his majesty move up against the pestle.
Today's elders dance the Apirede, but like children
Do not know when to stop;
Obra! Obra! Abusua and Ntoro gather, gather
It's about us, it's about our home
And it is about time!

They kill Piesie, kill Preko
They kill Sunsum, (they fixed- the evil eye on us)
And still they kill

Ambushed us between Azania and Oguaa, Oguaa and Wa.
O Tano, preserve us; keep us, keep us great Pra
Keep us, seed in your husk
Husk within amulet beneath your brass bed
Let the family grow in clusters, in clusters.
This is my first trip to sunrise, the farthest destination
Take me, first born, to your innumerable self
The seed sunk deep; Odum, take root
Borebore, unleash the spirit of war
Then we can pray in peace here at home

Deep in the knowledge
That at the shrine of the foolish
The wise assume nothing
But the need for scorn.

Kojo Laing

Born in Kumasi, Ghana, in 1946, Kojo Laing was educated in both Ghana and Scotland, taking an MA degree at Glasgow University. He spent nine years as an administrator in districts in Ghana and one year at the seat of government in Accra. He was made Secretary of the Institute of African Studies at the University of Ghana in 1980. Kojo Laing is presently a Chief Executive of a private school, St. Anthony's, founded by his mother in 1962.

Kojo Laing has published two novels, *Search Sweet Pountry*, and *Woman of the Aeroplanes*. He recently published an intriguing collection of poems, *Godhorse*.

Steps

The big man in *batakari*
with roses in his mouth
        feels
he is so important
that one step for him
        is
        a hundred for others,
            one smile
        a thousand laughs,
            one death
        a million slaughters.
Really big:
and one itch countless
            scratches.

Three songs

1   Bishop

        Guest to his own fears,
Bishop rises to God, with fly in his mouth,

organ bruises him with sad songs.
Bishop afraid to speak out against the world.
in case blessed fly flies out
      onto all manner of decent people.
As time goes, courage comes gently.
Bishop gives up hobnobbing with mighty and rich.
Fly comes out
to the consternation of the faithful;
and now he walks the same lonely road as me,
      where a candle joins the sun and the moon.
Bishop bishop,
      God sends you back down fighting and fighting.

2   Judge

Big judge watches big elephant
lose its tail and find a comma instead.
Surprised judge fences the sunlight
      in consternation, with legal wood.
        Court crowded with elephants searching
        for new tails to be given only by judge.
        Leaves fall and break
        with the heart of the judge.
Yes elephants carry his cloak
and po... at the accused with their trunks,
and as judge falls like a bishop in prayer.
The court of the heart is in uproar,
legal hands raised in inner agony
as wisdom attacks with wicked
      illogical intensity: life is what you make it
when elephants are around.
Judge judge,
you sail out of the court like a boat in danger,
you run to the house of your girl
whose arms break the fence
      and let the sun stun the eyes.
Judge goes to court every morning on elephant,
whose comma is triumphantly full of blood and skin.

3   Minister

Well powdered
          expansive
              tribal in the mornings,
Minister likes guavas,

but considers that each stone inside
may one day sabotage the skin.
Sun streaks through executive instruments
        and each ends up in Parliament
            where it finds that the moon has been repealed.

Sun burns the tongues of chatty politicians
        whose words scatter thinly across the land,
        and fertilize brilliantly
            all the cassava that needs them.

High powdered
                expensive
            regal in the evenings.
Minister likes butter but...

Atukwei Okai

Born in 1941 in Accra, Ghana, Atukwei Okai received his early education there and went on to the Gorky Literary Institute in Moscow, Soviet Union, where he obtained an MA in Literature. He also took an MPhil at the University of London. In 1978, he attended the International Writing Programme at Iowa.

Atukwei Okai has lectured in a number of universities but he has generally remained loyal and committed to the University of Ghana at Legon, where he taught literature and Russian. He is a past president of the Ghana Association of Writers and is a founder and current Secretary-General of the Pan African Writers Association (PAWA) which has its headquarters in Accra.

Among his books are *Flowerfall, The Oath of the Fontomfrom, Rhododendrons in Donkeydom, Lorgoligi Logarithms,* and some children's books. Atukwei Okai is a poet of great humour and indeed a .'living poem' himself. Apart from Kofi Awoonor, Atukwei Okai is perhaps the most famous and influential Ghanaian poet of his generation.

Watu Wazuri
(to B. B. Attuquayefio)

I

When all the blue is gone out of the sky
and the remaining hue is nothing to fly a kite by,

birdsong
is the green lawn
of spring

on which the ears laze,

Upon the nile of my soul,
the lullaby of the flutist

floats

I like a kite at dawn.

Ray Charles
and Stevie Wonder

you are acquainted with the
laughter of the thunder

but not with the look and
the smile of her lightning

that will meander

like the singing leap-year spine
of the sexy celestial belly dancer.

Like a Bobodiulasso kite
commissioned by the Supreme Council

of the clouds
and the moonlight
and the ten toes and ten fingers
of the horizon of the soul,
you only wander and wonder—

you do not see
the world
you sing about.

Waumbaji,**
Waumbaji
Watu Wazuri-
Rhododendrons in donkeydom.

II

Beethoven
Beethoven

you do not hear the songs
you sing about the world

you see.

Waumbaji,
Waumbaji
Watu Wazuri—
Rhododendrons in donkeydom.

III

Miriam Makeba...
Miriam Makeba...

She shall not savour
the air and the soil of the land
that fuels and fires
her soul into song.

Miriam Makeba,

her spirit shall never waver.
Lonely in the cave-canyon-kraal
of labour.

her soul seasonally floats home,
stealthily sucks
of her motherland's
midnight breasts,

bursts forth into new births of song,

steeling the spirit
of her people
panting and prancing

in the dormant
volcano-dungeon
of racialist dung
and human wrong.

Waumbaji,
Waumbaji
Watu Wazuri—
Rhododendrons in donkeydom.

IV

Osagyefo Kwame Nkrumah,

> O spirit on an errand,
> O spirit on an errand,

no sooner had you folded your mat
and gone beyond the corn-fields

than the victoria falls
the namib desert
and the table mountain

burst out
in tears
and fire,

and the towncrier and his gong
and the eagle soaring in flight
burst out into fight and into song,
guinea bissau, angola—
mozambique, angola—
guinea bissau, angola—
mozambique, angola—
A LUTA CONTINUA***
A LUTA CONTINUA
Waumbaji,
Waumbaji
Watu Wazuri—
Rhododendrons in donkeydom.

*   Swahili phrase for 'beautiful people'.
** Swahili word for 'Creators'.
***Portuguese expression for 'the struggle continues'.

Jonice

Sleep
    not
        on the sleeping
Wall—
        come sleep

On my shoulder;
           why do
You
    prefer
The wall
    to my human
Shoulder? it
May be coldly
         tall, but
I am
    near
And fonder;
      I have sent
You
    the call,
        wishing to
Be
    the sole
Holder
    of the head
          that
Will fall
     from
Your neck
    whose moulder
         has
Given
    me
You—
    and all
      for now till
When
    we grow
Older;
    sleep not
      on the
Sleeping wall—
Come sleep on my shoulder.

Kobena Eyi Acquah

Born in Winneba, Ghana, where he grew up, Kobena Acquah studied at the University of Ghana and the Ghana Law School. He is currently the Chief Legal Adviser to the Bank for Housing and Construction in Accra, Ghana.

Kobena Acquah is a Fellow of the Ghana Association of Writers, and has been at different times the Association's Editor, General Secretary, and Legal Adviser. He served on the Executive Board of the Ghana Book Development Council, and was also a Member of Ghana's 1979 Constituent Assembly.

He has received several international and national awards, including the University of Ghana Langston Hughes Prize (1974), the Valco Fund Literary Award (1977), Honourable Mention in the Noma Award (1985), Africa Area Award of the Commonwealth Poetry Prize (1985), and the Ghana Book Award (1986). He has published two poetry collections, *The Man Who Died* and *Music for a Dream Dance*.

I want to go to Keta

I want to go to Keta
before it is washed away,
before the palm trees wither
and drown outside the bay.

I want to go to Keta
where boys drum all the day
and the girls dance *agbadza*
to keep the tears away.

I want to go to Keta.
while yet they live who care
to point out like a star
that frothing spot out there

where they would sit with *dada*
those days the sea was land.
I want to go to Keta

while yet there's place to stand.

I want to go to Keta
before the tenderness
of grief so keen and bitter
chills to cold callousness

and the vagueness of laughter
drowns the shared joy of pain.
I want to go to Keta--
it might not long remain.

Tears

Have you as yet found an answer
to the question of tears?

At first I tried to ignore them,
then failing, to walk out on them and
shut the door behind me.
But I seem somehow to come back.

I suppose there is something about tears
that will always bring a man back;
whether as rivulets trickling down
the pain-carved valleys of the face,
or cataracts of gushing brine
inflaming their source, defying damming.

Tears are an argument
I'm yet to find an answer to.

When will you come again

When will you come again
from far off Africa?
When will you come again
and bring us banana?

Until that day they had never
seen skin as black as ours
except from drawings in their books
and what their teachers said.

Meeting us on their first visit
to a city museum,
they gazed in timid wonderment
and then ventured to ask:
When will you come again?

Not knowing if we could come back
or when, we offered them
something better than banana.

We told them of the little boys
and girls of Africa,
and then gave each one
a warm smiling handshake —
our love from Africa.

Wedding Wreaths

Mother must have thought it odd
To see wreaths
At a wedding feast—
Wreaths
At a time of rejoicing?

Lovely rings of
Forget-me-nots
White, yellow, pink.
And in the centre, roses.

Wreaths are for the dead,
Are they not,
To bestow love
And tender thoughts of bliss?

Mother must have thought it queer
Thought I—
Who heard of Pompeii's garlands
And the leis of Hawaii—
I was not supposed to.

And then, isn't marriage, after all,
A death of self?

Blue Danube

The Danube then must have been blue
When Strauss waltzed on enchanted airs
And village swallows Liszted vespers.

But when we got to see its flow
The Danube was a dull green glow
With golden sunrays glittering
Like jewels on its rippling tide.

We cruised in comfort down its length
and heard tales told from Visegrad woods
And thought how Buda bonbons were
As good as any anywhere.

We watched the campers by their fires
And sportsmen angling on the banks.
We felt at ease to rhyme verses.

Suddenly from the upper deck
Floated down from someone's radio
Psalm one hundred and thirty-seven
And nostalgia replaced our joy.

There on the Danube's moonlit miles
We seemed to feel the strange eyes stare
And foreign tongues wakened in us
A longing for the streams of home—

Ayeitsu, Tano, Densu, Pra,
And Volta with its mangrove swamps
By which to sit and sing our songs.

A Broken Egg

You said
if I gave you my heart
you would graft it into your own;
you would clutch firmly to my love
snug in your big, possessive fist,

never, never letting go.

And you
said you would be tender;
like an egg, the egg of your eye,
you would cuddle my life in yours,
and be true even beyond death.

And I
seemed to see in your eyes
the seal of all your promises;
I, needing someone just like you
to whom to surrender my all.

So now
dropped hard unto the ground,
shattered, and spilling out my fluid—
my yolk, my albumen, my life--
into the dust beneath your feet

I look
up to seek in your eyes
some sign that I will somehow live,
that you will pick up the pieces
and glue them together again
and pour your life back into mine.

But no,
your eyes just cannot see
into mine;
your eyes, tender and trusting once,
now broken,
blinded,
beyond love.

V- Y Okpoti Odamtten

Born in Kumasi, Ghana, in 1952, Okpoti Odamtten had his secondary school education in Ghana and England before taking both BA and MA degrees in English at the University of Cape Coast, Ghana. His PhD in English was at the State University of New York at Stony Brook.

He has taught at the University of Cape Coast, and at the State University of New York at Old Westbury. Okpoti Odamtten is presently an Assistant Professor of English at Hamilton College, New Yolk.

In 1977, he received the Valco Literary Prize, Ghana. And apart from publishing his poems in the *The Greenfield Review* and doing some literary criticism, Okpoti Odamtten has completed his book of poems, *Metsaka's Kente of Words*. Kofi Awoonor, the noted Ghanaian writer, has written very favourably about the former's poetry in Richard Priebe's *Ghanaian Literatures*.

For those in Ussher Fort: from the Beach at Elmina

(for Kosi, Kwaku and Comrades)

if only
if only the python would swallow
me whole:
    the rat thrust into darkness
if only
for those in Ussher Fort
Gideon's comfort cannot last
till dawn steals through the bars

for those who have heard sounds
heard sounds of cockroaches

between the bed and wall
between the body and bed
for those who have heard
more than the rat thrust into darkness
i confess my secret:
> about midnight a hunger gnaws me
> in my dreams of *gari*
> even without water, without sugar
> without knowing how it is
> for you who always wake to my dreams
> as the morning creeps into your cell ...

if only
if only the python could swallow the noise
if only
for those who have heard the sounds
of early morning seagulls singing
the songs of flight, hovering
> beyond the bars
the wind whips the waves to pound
against Ussher Fort.

yet i must confess:
> these waves sound pleasant here
> weaving with these words
> you cannot hear that i must hear here
> thrust into the darkness
> i hear
> nothing,

but
those in Ussher Fort have always heard music
> at night ...

To the Spirit of a Jay-Jay*

You stood, or should we say
perched
from the railings
a little *akasanoma*
us into actions
which were only reactions
for we had heard
only too well these songs

of praise and blame
to blunt the rising venom,
the rising voices wanting
wanting ...

MILITARY UPRISING—SAVIOURS OF OUR
    SOCIETY!
Hail
the disen's bloody rays
bullet across the nation
glorious promise of Democracy's
satisfaction cannot be realized
now
is time to think
violence
                is necessary
only because of this
                creation's poverty
which hears your voices
asking: how we are forever
in this seeming eternity of wanting?

though we are all together
some of us have PROPERTY
to protect
though we are all together
some of us have...
hopes unvoiced, sacrificed in the
cajoling, bullying, pleading song
you trill from your perch
like *akasanoma* about to fly
again, please do not
SHIT ON US...

*Written to mark the 4 June military uprising led by Flt. Lieutenant Jerry J. Rawlings in
Ghana.

On seeing Theresa: A choral dirge

Theresa, o
Theresa, o
your eyes scream
a fire that glows
in the dying embers

of our family

Nana Theresa
whose kindness did
not kill her,
whose kindness gave
her a lot of trouble...

Nana Theresa
who grew old
before her youth had
danced forty festivals

Nana Theresa
whose kindness did
not kill her,
whose kindness gave
her a lot of trouble...

Nana Theresa asking how
can she neglect
her sacred duties:
child growing the daughter
daughter flowering the wife
wife opening into mother
mother scattering herself to sell
the new life she dreamed
for her tired bones
can only be the dream
in the ashes
of our family.

Accusations...One More Time

(the flagellants)

> kramo-bone amma
> yanhu kramo-pa*

and when we met
I did not, no
I did not know
YOU

and when we met

your words were mangoes
were mangoes ripe
to burst their sweetness
over virgin lips
juice running over my tongue
when we met
yes I do and
I did ..

now you say
now you say harshly
like the taste of bitter-leaf
the soup was cooked
on another's fire
        and your words are flames
        deep within my womb

when you say
my gourd, once your delight,
is filled with bitter-leaf
and another has taken
the he-goat's testicles
he-goat's testicles from the soup

but now we meet
do you
do you think
that I must carry
this legacy this memory — image of you
I did not know
I did not no
I did not know
this life, this daymare
ever present
would remind me so
remind me of you...

*We are deceived because the charlatan's potions resemble the healer's medicine; or,
because of hypocrisy, the fake and the genuine look alike.

Guinea-Bissau

Ampa

Jorge Ampa

Born on 28 August, 1950 in Bolama, Guinea-Bissau, Jorge Ampa had his early education in Bissau and later in Portugal.

He has travelled extensively to such places as Poland, Cuba, Ethiopia, Soviet Union, Morocco, and Spain. Apart from publishing poems in various anthologies and journals, he contributes articles often to such publications as *No Pintcha* and serves on the editorial board of *Revista Internacional* of the Portuguese language (RILP).

When A Child Does Something

A child does not discriminate by colour:
The colour he has
Is the one others have.
He feels the pain
Provoked by lack of love.

Towards a child,
One should not show rancour.

When he cries,
Know he is a victim
Of a heart of pebbles.

When he does something,
Someone is
At the base of it.

When he hurts another child
In his common world
Of childish innocence,
It is because he sees in him
A copy of another abuse.
He understands

In his own way
His usurped rights.

A child should be protected
From adults' skunk behaviour.
A child never forgets
And neither ignores his weakness
In defence of his rights.
At least, his rights,
He watches and waits. Grows...
And when he receives love and attention,
He is grateful,
Profoundly.
Even when he does not speak.

Impressions

They exist in themselves.
First and last, they are always impressions.

Their manifestation is like something
One translates
In different and opposing exclamations
Of the phenomenon of
"I have seen you before, yes. But I don't
Know where?"
Or "I have the impression that..."

Impressions, remote memories
Transcending each impact, that awakes
Each image which we incorporate
As standard...
They are intrinsic.

It is like they were born in us,
Including dreams.

Cote d'Ivoire

Ebony. Tadjo

Noel Ebony

Born in Tanokoffikro, Ivory Coast, in 1944. Like the African poet, David Diop, he died in July 1986 on Mount Mamelles in Dakar, Senegal. In his short but productive life, he was only able to publish one book, *Déjà vu*.

(Untitled- *editor*)

who knows the country where I come from
this country of stupor
with the marks of red flesh
this country with bizarre decrees
this country with busts of tears in the abyss
who knows
the whips that I have endured
the humiliation I have drunk
who knows
the prayers that I have uttered
the hatred that I have harboured
the love which made me desperate
the winters which my soul has suffered
who knows the country where I come from
the bitter country of the agile anaconda
you who know this country
praise with me
the battalion of the standing heart
the battalions of hope

siege with me
fortresses of the masters of the night
ring ring
horns and koras
tam-tam attoungblan with a clouded beard
tell the country where I come from
the country which stretches itself with languid joys
which undulates

the country where *konvoo anokye* the old
tied the palmtree
the country where sunjata* the great
uprooted the fromager tree
roll
the thunders and trumpets
fence
lords of war
empty the voodoo and ndoep
yes
ring
horns and koras
wave with your rich *onomatopoeia*
on forgetful memories

*A thirteenth century king of the West African empire of Mali who, though a cripple, was
a man of great bravery who defeated his rival, Sumaguru Kanteh.

Véronique Tadjo

Born on 21 July, 1955 in Cote d'Ivoire, she has published a collection of poems called *Laterite* which was awarded a literary prize by L'Agence de Coopération Culturelle et Technique in 1983. Veroniique Tadjo has also published a novel,*A vol d'oiseau*.

(Untitled- Editor)

LIFE IS MADE UP OF
BLACK THISTLES AND THORNS
I WOULD HAVE WANTED IT
SWEETER AND LESS BITTER
BUT AS YOU KNOW
THE LIMIT OF THINGS
SETS BACK EACH MOMENT
FACES ARE CHANGED
AND LOVERS OPPRESS
ONE ANOTHER
YOU KNOW VERY WELL
IN THE NIGHT OF YOUR TERROR
ONLY YOU EXIST (YOU ALONE EXIST)

OVER THERE, PEOPLE
LIVE WITH MANY MANY SECRETS
AND THE BREATH OF GRASSLANDS
WHISTLES ALONG THE ROAD
INTERTWINED WITH PATHS,
THE GREY SKY BECOMES BLUE
AND THE FLUTE THAT YOU HEAR
IS COMING DIRECTLY
FROM PORO

I HAVE A DREAM
OF A LITTLE GIRL
WITH DARK EYES
AND THICK HAIR
WHOM I WOULD LOVE
VERY MUCH
AND WHO WOULD HAVE MY SKIN
A LITTLE GIRL
WITH CHEEKS LIKE MANGOES
AND TINY FINGERS
I HAVE A DREAM
IN MY WOMB
GESTATION (PREGNANCY)
FOR THE FIRST TIME
THE OBSESSION

SUDDENLY
TIME HALTS
AND THE TIC-TAC OF TIME
ROARS LIKE A TOM-TOM
HER HAIR ON THE PILLOW
SING A MELANCHOLY SONG
SUDDENLY
DECEPTION INVADES THE CITY
AND YOUR HAND
ON HER HAND
THEY TRY TO COMMUNICATE
YOUR BODY MOVES FROM SIDE TO SIDE
HER CHEEK IS MOIST
THE NIGHT IS YET TO START
BUT FOR YOU
IT IS THE END
OF A VERY IMPORTANT RENDEZ-VOUS

Liberia

Uzo

Uzo

Born in 1966, he is a Nigerian/Liberian poet presently living in New York city. He has written three collections of poetry: *immunity, Imago, and Marine Cemetery, as well as an experimental novella, Second Childhood.*

In addition to receiving several awards for his poetry, Uzo has received a National Arts Club Literary Award and an Academy of American Poets Student Prize (1990).

Dawn of the Solitary Walker

a calm moon anchored in mist
sinks
to a world of trees.
through air's ethereal womb
dawn emerges
its ghost-blue head.
beneath a vague skin
i am silent.
yellow breath of wind from the Hudson
and a shadow appears on a wall.
calm figure approaching:
my conscience?
or the soul's distant accomplice
of a crime forever committed:

          FEAR

Oasis

I have abandoned
    my body

I have abandoned
            illusions
pressed
by a rising tide of
                nightmares
like a flight of bats
I emerge through my cave of bones ...

Skies lined with hooks
take my mind to distances
as I pass scentless across the borders of reason,
then through
the blind ears of spirits breathing shadows
speaking truths
in silences blind as our
lives
as winds rise to orchestras swelling the air in a thickly
tendoned timbre of harps and weeping of melting trumpets.

I am the imago of the world...

Pressed
by the conditions of my life
I am borne across the barren limits of the soul
breathless
I sit and drink my thoughts
from lagoonal bones and fish for truths in silences.

Factory

Dream that has raised me above the jungles of sleep
night that has allowed me to rest in her silver palms
            above disappearing forests
silence and my fear slipping its chains into the void ...
Virtues and deceptions still gliding along the conveyer
            belts of history
equation of-an entire people
            still functioning
minds sailing like ghosts
            through factories of thought.
Black People:
What long blade is buried in your breast
        what flaming wound do you still endure

what wind still steers the fragrant pollution into
      the broad masts of your pride
in what dark bay do serpents of your
        anger sleep with voices of ancestors
           submerged in the storm
and what view across the hilltops
        will be reinvented
by the coming dawn.

Sleep

This night

time-clocks filled with ghosts feast on
vampiric silences.
I run my hands across my ribs'
blue hills and wade through the dark lakes of my skin.

This night

houses are burning
in the rising fires of my earthen secrets
convictions
like frightened children
sprint leagues beyond my night of smoking hills...

Night passes

time-clocks fade
into themselves like the breath of ghosts

an earthen musk wakens from my skin ...

A scent of pleasant deaths.
The renewal of the soul in sleep.

Mali

Ouologuem

Yambo Ouologuem

Born on 28 August, 1940 in Bandiagara, the Dogon country of Mali. He spent his early academic years in Bamako before proceeding to Paris in 1962 to study literature, philosophy and sociology.

His first novel, *Le Devoir de Violence* (Bound to Violence), won the prestigious Prix Renaudot in 1968. Later he published a satirical pamphlet,*Lettre ouverte à la France-negre,* addressed to General de Gaulle. Sundry publications of poems in magazines and anthologies followed.

To my Husband

Your name used to be Bimbircokak
And everything was fine that way
But you became Victor-Emile-Louis-Henri-Joseph
And bought a table set

I used to be your wife
And you called me your august-half
We used to eat together
And you reared us around the table

Calabash and scoop-spoons
Gourd and *kous-kous*
Disappeared from the oral menu
That my paternal commandment dictated

We are modern, you used to say
And you used to drink the respect of my sight clear and confident

Hot, hot is the sun
At the demands of the tropics
But your tie does not leave
Your neck threatened by strangulation

And since you ignore me when I speak of Negritude
Oh yes, let's talk about western servitude
But please, look at me
How do you find me?

We will eat grapes, pasteurized milk, spiced bread,
All imported
And eat little
In private like knowledgeable people say
it is not surprising if
'A fric"
Means Africa without money

Your name used to be Bimbircokak
And everything was fine that way
You wanted to be Victor-Emile-Louis-Henri-Joseph
Which
As far as I could remember
Does not recall your parentage with
Rocquefort
(Old cheese branch coming from Rocquefort
and other fetishes)
But you see Bimbircokak
By your fault of being a fanatic of forks and spoons
From underdeveloped, I became undernourished

Fric is a French slang for "money".

When Negro Teeth Speak

Everyone thinks me a cannibal
But you know how people talk

Everyone sees my red gums but who
Has white ones
Up with tomatoes

Everyone says fewer tourists will come
Now
But you know
We aren't in America and anyway everyone
Is broke

Everyone says it's my fault and is afraid
But look
My teeth are white not red
I haven't eaten anyone

People are wicked and say I gobble
The tourists roasted
Or perhaps grilled
Roasted or grilled I asked them
They fell silent and looked fearfully at my gums
Up with tomatoes

Everyone knows an arable country has agriculture
Up with vegetables

Everyone maintains that vegetables
Don't nourish the grower well
And that I am well grown for an undeveloped man
Miserable vermin living on tourists
Down with my teeth

Everyone suddenly surrounded me
Fettered
Thrown down prostrated
At the feet of justice

Cannibal or not cannibal
Speak up
Ah you think yourself clever
And try to look proud

Now we'll see you get what's coming to you
What is your last word
Poor condemned man

I shouted up with tomatoes

The men were cruel and the women curious you see
There was one in the peering circle
Who with her voice rattling like the lid of a casserole
Screamed
Yelped
Open him up
I'm sure papa is still inside

The knives being blunt

Which is understandable among vegetarians
Like the Westerners
They grabbed a Gillette blade
And patiently
Criss
Crass
Floccc
They opened my belly

A plantation of tomatoes was growing there
Irrigated by streams of palm wine
Up with tomatoes

The Crazy Heart

Shut up or I scream
I am asking for your forgiveness
But the solitude
The solitude of dereliction
Do you know what is a life of solitude

At the crazy speed of my heartbeat
Alone to pluck the hoofs of unreal weight
To untie bundles of rose buds
To blow an azure flute-tormented with the unknown
Oh yes
Yes, of course
I know what you think

With your hugging thigh made of breeze
You animate the velvet of my scared pollens
Which speaks which chats
And say that I am making it up

Kneeling in front of your body where the night freezes
The dirty grey of my sinful shadow draws a cross
And I cry
Oh yes
Breathless nudity
I have seen you, me, in the darkness where boiled
The forests which have lost their mast of desires

I am not crazy
You kissed him

Shut up or I scream
I ask for your forgiveness
My craziness abandons itself
In the whisper of roses

I have raised this
Forgetting the sacred commandments
I have raised this
Just to intimidate you
My two heavy hands conquered by perjury
When suddenly...no...moan/shiver
I have glued to your dead eyelids
The broken petals of unnecessary noises which prayed
Shut up offerings of my madness
Rest in peace, my love

Mauritania

Taleb-Khyar

Mohammed B. Taleb-Khyar

Born on 24 July 1963 in Atar, Mauritania, Mohammed Taleb-Khyar grew up in Nouakchott, the capital. He did his studies in France where he earned a Maitrise in English Literature from University of Orleans. He then moved to the University of Virginia, USA., to complete his PhD in French. He is now an Assistant Professor of French at Tufts University in Massachusetts, USA.

Taleb-Khyar serves on the editorial board of *Callaloo, a* journal of African and African-American arts and letters, published at the University of Virginia. He recently published with Charles Rowell, chief editor of *Callaloo,* an article titled, "African Studies: An Annual Annotated Bibliography" and does also occasional translation.

Imagine the Rain

No, it is not that;
The boy is sound of mind.
First, among his friends,
The desert knows him,
And also the pen.
At seven, he knows how to prepare tea;
He knows his *Sourat*,* knows his *Jarrum***.
He just would not believe it.
His mother, his uncle, and I
Told him. He would not believe.
Not even that water, sweet
Brown water comes from the sky.
He would not believe it.
Is it the rare resilience of youth?
I do not know.
He asks, "Who pours water
From the sky?" Sahara-eyes
Intent for answers.

"God does, you little heathen!
"Does He choose to pour it
On one person?"
My uncle said, no;
He saw one of the horns of the stag
Shining wet; the other dry.
"Can you see God's hand

Pouring water from the sky?"
"Can you see His bucket?"

I tucked my mouth
Under my turban.
I have no need to fear the rain.

*Sourat: a Qur'anic chapter.
* *Jarrum: an Arabic grammar book in verse learned by heart.

Niger

Watta. Harouna

Oumarou Watta

Born on 14 January, 1951 in Gaya, Niger Republic, he attended the Lycee Nationale in Niamey, Niger, and the Ecole Normale at Zinder, where he received a teaching diploma. He continued his studies at the Université de Niamey where he received his bachelors degree. He has attended Universities at Colchester, England, and the State University of New York in Albany where he received his PhD.

Oumarou Watta has taught at the University of Niamey and is presently teaching at the University of New Orleans at Lake Front.

He has published a book of poems, *In-Sign-E,* which merges the traditional proverbs and thought-patterns of the Hausa and Zarma-Songhay languages of the people of Niger with his own mastery of English.

Handy Dogs

> *-Ha nsi, may ni ga donda?*
> *-Iri koara kaa ko.*
> (Zarma-Songhay)

Whosoever dislikes his host
Or guest is less than mister dog
He is asked whom he hates
Most
He retorts him who visits
His master's abode
There lies the law
Of good nature
Neighbours erect fences
And the howl of hounds
Host their sleep
Nature works
On man a trick

To make man a dog
Eating dog

Make-Up

E wande Fatuma
Nda tun way kurey
A ma gwandi te sasey
A ma nagi te cirau
A ma dan te korbey
Ka mo nialau-nialau ...

Lingering in lust
With sweet memories of days past
She makes a collar of a cobra
She makes eye-lotion of hemlock
She makes a ring of a scorpion
She brushes her eye-brows with an earthworm
Sweeps here, sweeps there
Brushes here, brushes there
Brown cross in kowa-gold circle
Out of a mussel shell mixture
Rubs, dulls, draws doe eye
That grazes on grass of grace
And rolls and rolls two white rocks
And rocks and rocks two youthful hills
And sways and sways waving fibres
Under hands of lustful breezes
In the heat of her smooth face
Her breath moves the leaves
In the triple pattern
Of embracing flickering figures
She who chews tobacco flower
In the midst of roaring stream
A glass in her brown petals at sunset
To woo winds and wed waves
Digs roots in a swamp of beauty.

Abdoulaye Djibo Harouna

Born on 29 November, 1957 in Niamey, Niger. He did his undergraduate studies in General Literature at the University of Niamey and then continued on for his masters degree in Comparative Literature at Pennsylvania State University. He completed his PhD in the same area of specialization at Pennsylvania State.

Abdoulaye Harouna has published poems in periodicals such as *Ufahamu*.

The Message
(To Ngugi wa Thiong'o)

valiant warrior
Exile-weary
Yet resolute
On your lonely
Path
Sometimes I wonder
HOW
You do it?

Voice
Above the silence
Sometimes I sit
And ponder
WHY
You do it?

Until
One restless night
When sleep is scarce
You came to me
  Child,
  I refuse to die

for it is suicidal
not to
FIGHT.

Immortality

(To David Diop, who even in his grave defies Death)

Oh! You
food for worms,
flickering twinkle of light
if you wish to flame
now and forever
hearken to the voice
of Truth
heed to the secret
of time:
the future is
but now and yesterday

So Serve,
Serve,
Serve Humanity
and you will live
for an eternity.
Live,
Live,
Live for others
and you will live forever!

Senegal

Ndao. Gueye. Wara. Sall

Cheikh Ndao

Born in Karthiack, near Bignona, Senegal, his full name is Sidi Ahmed Alioune Cheikh Ndao. He had his high school education in Dakar and continued his higher studies in France. He attended the University of Grenoble in France and also went to a university in Britain, at Swansea. Presently, he is a professor of English at L'Ecole Normale William Ponty in Thies.

Cheikh Ndao has won several literary awards and honours, including the Senegalese prize for poetry in the French language in 1962 for his collection of poems, *Kairée. A* partisan or defender of transcription and the use of African languages, he writes in Wolof, French, and English.,

A master of several literary genres: poetry, fiction, drama, Ndao has published two books of poems, Kairée and *Mogariennes:* two novels, *La Marabout de la Secheresse* and *Excellence! You Wives;* and a play, *L'exil D'Aboury.*

Ndeysan*

My sails are at the command of your breath
Up to the roots of your eyebrows
Where I am staggering beaten by Noon
Which outlines our shadows

Ah imagine my path
Along the blue island of your lips
To the shores of reeds of incense
And perfumed pearls

When the storm is calmed down
The waves will unroll their braided hair
For the Lover of those keeping watch
Let me be the sand of the shore
Whose dust blows into your pores

*Ndeysan: a term in Wolof meaning "What a pity."

Tears

Mother of rape and burglary
Am I going to light my tears of fire
This steep descent
Toward the abyss of my horrors
O you the hosts
No guests
Centenary vultures

For me my crown of termites and mites
You shall I say Friends
From the depth of my heart
These daily visits
Are from hyenas that reigned like queens

O son
Now barricade up to my feet
The dusty dawn of Bambouk's thousand spangles
At the cross-roads of my blood
The furious fiery horses of olden days
I illumined my spirit
The royal path of Biram's son
Holding the bridle of Guilé's lion
Of Mouk-Mouk at Macina

Ah! I am fed up with the reed pens of scribes
From the East and the West
Whose fingers scribble
And who crouch to the glory of my name
My motherly hands lay on your head

Kankan Moussa
You
Who did not kneel down
Before the commander of believers

Those who stink the fear of prisons
Are not on my horizon
Those who toast to prosperity
Of the owners
Exploiting their own people
Are not on my horizon

My loin-cloths belong to the Wrestlers

Call the winners
Of Dimbokoro
To the creaking filaos
Of Thiaroye
My tom-tom for funerals
That I carry with flowery skin hiccups
Since dawn spewed out its glowing embers
On the surprising tents

They will drink my calabash gourd of honey
    You
      Kenyatta
In your solitary castle
Watch the gaiters and iron helmets
Grinning behind the barbed wire
    You
      Kwame
To my right
in the circle of Adopted Sons
    You
Wolof child of Rufisque
Imagine the sunset
At Seumbdioun
On your dark windows
Beautiful gaolo of Podor
That creeps toward my insanity
The joyous rhythm of koras and sabars
Daughter of lightning
And sunny waters
Into your calabashes falls
The rain without name
From the flesh greenish desire
Sufficient to your body
And this sky full of doves
Will cover the clouds of our grief

Landscape

Where are my mounds reddened
    by the wounds of the sun
      my hills tilled with termites
      and ants

Accompanied me on the journeys
    my dreams
    play hide and seek
    with children of the dusk

Where are my baobab trees that hold
    the sky
My baobabs are stronger
    than invincible Doussouba

Suddenly now pines as lean as famished
    Tukolor imams
Bend toward the East
    in their evening salam

Pines
    calm and solitary
    like Peul shepherds who have no flock

Don't be moved by the tears of the star
    that is dying
    inside the tentacles of octopus
    Pensive pines

Are those your companions
    willows weeping and whispering
    like widows of the Emir
    in front of Atar's tent

    Beautiful mourners
The cohort
    of heraldic clouds
    of azure fragments
    of contemptuous distributing angels
    Is rushing around
    Waw o
It is the season of adornment

    Beautiful mourners
Dry your tears
    the caress of Fall
    will dye your braids with henna
    and hang gold coins nests
    in your hair

You mischievous child
    from grasslands, seas, deserts
    lift up the Haik of my beautiful Bedouins
    I am the bee in search of pollen
    in the month of May

    Beautiful mourners
Gipsy dancers
    in the streets of Malaga
    the blackness of your eyes
    recall Koumba Laobe
    in the night of Korité

O! you can charm
    your carefree lords
    ibis looks at the flowing Nile
    but you look at your dwelling place
    these pagoda temples of Tonkin
    surrounded by trembling fir trees intoxicated with
    hail storm
Over there over there.

Silcarneyni Gueye

Born on 3 November, 1943 in Dakar, Senegal, he did commercial studies at Delafosse Technical Secondary School and proceeded to do his undergraduate work at Dakar University (now Cheikh Anta Diop University), where he also received a Masters degree in Public Law and Political Science. He also did two years of studies at the National School of Administration of Senegal, ending with a postgraduate degree of Counsellor of Foreign Affairs.

Gueye is primarily a career diplomat who has served his country in several high-level diplomatic capacities in Ethiopia, Nigeria, Morocco, and Belgium. In Senegal, he has served as Assistant Director for political and cultural affairs and Chief of Africa Division in the Ministry of Foreign Affairs. He has also been a professor of diplomatic studies and of management at the National School of Administration of Senegal and the West African Centre for Monetary Studies of the Central Bank (based in Dakar) respectively.

He has published a book of poems titled, *Toi, je...* and has had works in an anthology of Senegalese poetry. He is currently a senior diplomat in the Senegalese Embassy, Washington DC.

Sermon of Twenty-One years

Today
Sunday 3 November 1963
I am twenty-one years
Twenty years of joys
and suffering
suddenly giving me
a sublime gift of
Heaven

Twenty years
Uncertainty and

brilliant prelude
Twenty years
Great ambition of poetic
passion

This silence
This heavy silence
of completed time
dawns on me
my heart beat is red
with blood
oh this sound
these sighs

Yes
I will brave the spirit of the past
that germinated in this heart
Hope and liberty

Manden Wara

Born in 1953 in Marsassoum, Cassamance region of Senegal, he attended Lycée Djignabo in Ziguinchor, still in the same region. He did his undergraduate work at the Université de Dakar (now Cheikh Anta Diop University), where he graduated with a degree in English. He went on further to take his MA and PhD at the University of California at Los Angeles.

Manden Wara is currently teaching in the French Department at the University of Virginia. He has published several critical articles, reviews, translations, and creative works in such publications as *Callaloo, Ufahamu,* and *Research in African Literatures.*

The Old Song (Rattle) of the Angry Man

To see you enjoying yourself
There is nothing to enjoy
Accra plateau
Sahara colourful light
Subdued night music

There is nothing to enjoy
To enjoy
Watching you enjoying yourself
But he is only a blazing dead wood
When your gazes coil like a serpent on a blazing branch
Rubbing itself
Wriggling
Twisting sluggishly
There is nothing to enjoy
Your big eyes painful back pale feverish face
swollen open lips look like a mango in the sun
red and ripe

To enjoy
watching you enjoying
In the subdued light
Joining body and soul
Coiled like a serpent
Rubbing like a snake
Burning like a snake
Mortified in his arms
It is nothing to enjoy

The Song of Nedjma

Kateb katib
You were verily to Nedjma
Ya habibi ya kateb ya
You were very true to Nejdma
Leila Nedjma
Very loving to Nedjma
Only to care for Nedjma

The sun has pity on us
the night
And you are as beautiful as this
Summer night
And your son, the lion's søn is neither grass-eating nor
  jackal, he can't even be ugly
And your house is not a real home, an oasis, a lover, a
heavenly gate
Your zeal, your zeal for generosity
And your powerful voice
You were very dear to Nedjma
Ya habibi ya kateb
And you mock at the folly of those whose trembling hands
became shrivelled
And you curse the fetid breath of injustice
But in front of Nedjma your dull eyes set ablaze
your mouth blossoms your watery nostrils smell the nectar
of evening roses

To love Nedjma
To seduce Nedjma
To conquer Nedjma

For you loved Nedjma
You smelt Nedjma
You laughed at Nedjma
You suffered like Nedjma
You lived like Nedjma
You' were Nedjma

And suddenly in the Spring of this plowed sky
The shining grain of maize
Ndeissane, it is the star of liberty,
Yacine!

From Tacfarinas, and Jugurtha
From Sétifs to Sétifs
You have been admiring Nedjma.

At the end of so long a journey, the morning star still returns
to sing your old refrain, your old song of love
Being in love with simple joy
Your heart burning with love, beats fast, panting furiously
Nedjma's love bursts out instantly with importance
Like a horse prancing and sweating before Aures
Nedjma's desire explodes at any moment
From Agadir to Babel Oued
From Atlas to Adrar
Your sensuous body crackles,
And with rage it hides under words

And things
"O devouring mother, domineering lover
Incorruptible Nedjma
Elusive Nedjma
You show your silhouette but never flank

But surrounded by arduous chains of tyranny, you saw
hard grains of violence whistling in the desert storm
moving sand, prisons full of people tortured, grounded and
engulfed in deep silence; prisons flourish with death,
wars with deadly weapons

But surrounded by arduous chains of tyranny, you yelled at us
although we were very exhausted, although our minds were confused,
the armistice of our hearts yelled:
"Stand firm, brothers and sisters, stand firm!
Nedjma is not far away

Nedjma is inviting us
For love, for liberty
Forward for Nedjma!"

Indefatigable helmsman, yelled and yelled:
"Oye, everybody, oye,!
We are born to live
Expel death from your minds
Forward Nedjma
For freedom."
And from the sword of Abdelkader

And from the pen of Abdelkader
You made a golden banner for Mandela
In the City of Nedjma
To construct
To erect
At the heart of the equator
Without a set square or compass
But with a single and ample gesture
O you, master geometry
Builders of pyramids
O you, the just, the tyrant! i salute you
With two hands joined together, and arms raised
Toward the midday sun and the Mediterranean.
The echo of your song was harmony, rhythm, life.
Then, at the cross-roads of time
The light of the sun and the morning star faded away
So that NEDJMA lives.

Amadou Lamine Sall

Born in 1951 in Kaolack, he did his higher education at the University of Dakar (now Cheikh Anta Diop University). The distinguished Senegalese former poet-president, Leopold Sedar Senghor, said that "...Amadou Lamine Sall is one of the most gifted of the second generation of Senegalese poets writing in the French language."

Sall has published three books of poems, *Mante des Aurores, Comme un Iceberg en Flammes,* and the latest *Locataire du neant,* which was given honourable mention in the 1990 Noma Award. Following on the footsteps of Senghor, Sall has co-edited with Charles Carrere a major anthology of the French-speaking poets of Africa titled, *Nouvelle Anthologie De La Poesie Negre Et Malgache.*

Letter To A Roving Poet

I don't know where you come from
what name you are so proud of
I don't know from what far away country you are the son
what type of hospitality you have adopted
I don't know whose mother or father
you resemble so much
I don't know what eternal dream you harbour
what solitary hostage you have become
I don't know 'at what horizon you seem to build your plans
from what love you allow deliverance
I don't know for whom
your heart bubbles with joy
I don't know of what memories you are captive
in what jail you live
I don't know what is your fate
what future you are the living dead

I don't know what heaven
which God
I don't k now what type of love
you are DOVE and eagle of fire
all that I must tell you
I LOVE YOU

Cloak of Dawn

I looked for you everywhere yet nowhere
Between the flower and the stalk
Between day and night
Among laughter of sleep
And the caress of the absent

Where are you daughter of the night
Now the poem is panting and words are scarce
The pen intoxicated with black wine dances arabesque
vowels are listless
While restive consonants wander in procession
On the empty page that yawns
You will be the only one to understand tonight why
I write this poem...

. . .

Now, when I see you again
You will tell me the time
And later you will tell me the time again
We shall go to buy newspapers of the right and the left
Left-right right-left

I will read them from the east to the west
You will comment on them from north to south
Then we shall disseminate news everywhere
At the four corners of the world of illiteracy and hunger
We shall then go to listen to the politicians

Of all stature and all colours
Very terrible and dangerous liars
. . .

For it seems that COMMUNISM is to be abolished for
peace on earth
CAPITALISM to be fought for peace on earth
SOCIALISM to be redefined for peace on earth
But not a single nation has an ideology called
LOVE

We shall live elsewhere
Because God seems to live elsewhere
. . .

I shall go with you by all available routes
To sow the first seeds of LIBERTY through suffering
We shall build cities without houses or streets
Without prisons or hatred
Where anonymous men without status will come to
 sleep
. . .

Manthie I would have loved to lie
To you that no little child is starving in the world
That no mother is crying for a wizened child contorted
by bomb
Of a quiet pilot
That no widow is tormented in front of a cadaver
Impossible to express any love
. . .

To lie to you
That nobody in exile suffers from terrible fear
To lie again and again Manthie that

No Apartheid
No Soweto
No Jones-town
No Red Brigade Army
No Black September
No Lebanon like an immense cake made with blood
No wandering people in a Palestine without home
No Israel whose history is persecutor being persecuted,
To lie to you
So that you never recognize their murderous hands

May God transform you into daughter of the night
And that I see tomorrow the candle flame of my people

And of the world
Burning at the Altar of great fate
Under the Arch of triple flower of LOVE
of PEACE
of LIBERTY

Sierra Leone

**Cheney-Coker. Hazeley. Johnson.
Peters. Fitzjohn.**

Svl Cheney-Coker

Born in 1945 in Freetown, Sierra Leone. He had his early education in Freetown and later went to universities in Oregon, California, and Wisconsin.

Cheney-Coker has taught at several universities, including the University of Maiduguri in Nigeria and a university in the Philippines. He has also been a drummer, a journalist, and a radio producer.

Among his works are four books of poetry: *The Road to Jamaica, Concerto for an Exile, The Graveyard also has Teeth,* and most recently, *Blood in the Desert's Eye.* He has also recently published a fantastic novel titled *The Last Harmattan of Alusine Dunbar.*

The Plague

Now to stop this desert encroaching upon my heart!

my Africa already diseased with its ubiquitous parasites
comes down with a fever and when the hurricane breaks
through the fragile veins of its body we glare at its ribs
the banana-riped putrefaction of its life

like cattle dying of rinderpest
the men who are dying of gangrene
the women who drink a bucketful of water
and wake up the next morning surprised at their river-blindness
and the heart of this continent pulsates at every attack
by its wolves, its womb where the blazing furnaces of the droughts
makes a bonfire of the carcasses of dead dreams
my Africa so long betrayed!

there is that part of her expanding tumour
that calls itself the giant of Africa

whose brain has fallen asleep
in whom lizards burrow into their holes
to escape the rotten smell of decay
when the galloping pestilences of our world
are magnified and where a cynical philosopher
teaches his disciples to say DOOM instead of BOOM

We play a deadly game!
the dethroned monarchs wait in the shadows
to unfurl their magic carpets once again
but these brothers who speak the language of the hour
what malady has eaten their brains
that they suck ruthlessly the breasts of a continent
shrivelling like the leaves of the oleander
in the relentless heat of our desert?

yesterday, I could have played the soothsayer
but who listens to Artemidoros these days?
There are already too many like him congesting our prisons.

Freetown*

Africa I have long been away from you
wandering like a Fulani cow
but every night
amidst the horrors of highway deaths
and the menace of neon-eyed gods
I feel the warmth of your arms
centrifugal mother reaching out to your sons
we with our different designs innumerable facets
but all calling you mother womb of the earth
liking your image but hating our differences
because we have become the shame of your race
and now on this third anniversary of my flight
my heart becomes a citadel of disgust
and I am unable to write the poem of your life

my creation haunts me behind the mythical dream
my river dammed by poisonous weeds in its bed
and I think of my brothers with 'black skin and white masks'
(I myself am one *heh heh heh*)
my sisters who plaster their skins with the white cosmetics

to look whiter than the snows of Europe
but listen to the sufferings of our hearts

there are those who when they come to plead
say make us Black Englishmen decorated Afro-Saxons
Creole** masters leading native races
but we African wandering urchins
who will-return one day
say oh listen Africa
the tom-toms of the revolution
beat in our hearts at night

make us the seven hundred parts of your race
stretching from the east to the west
but united inside your womb
because I have dreamt in the shadows of Freetown
crashing under the yoke of its ferocious civilization!

Freetown: the capital of Sierra Leone was founded as the mecca for the resettlement of
freed slaves; hence its name.
**Creole. descendants of freed slaves who were resettled in Freetown and the stock from
whom the poet hails.

Solitude

I am standing by a lake
watching the algae fondle with the swans
this purple heart within me I open my mouth
to sing the night the sad soprano of my life
my shadow my lake have you the solace I seek for the night

amidst the lake ten boats anchored lazily
bringing back my grief the memory of two hundred years
the passage bellowing inside me forcing my tears
oh Granville Sharpe,* have you come to plague this bleeding heart
again

my love my traitor my
callous aphrodite
I am no longer your Pushkin
I die no more for you
no sword in my hand
no duel in my heart
to guide me to my death coward between my legs

I save my tears for the swans
the night delivers me to my death
straight to the bar head in my rum
to drink my sorrows to the brink.

Granville Sharpe, an eighteenth century British philanthropist and abolitionist.

Peasants

'The Masters of the Dew'
- *Jacques Roumain*

The agony: I say their agony!

the agony of imagining their squalor but never knowing it
the agony of cramping them in roach-infected shacks the agony of treating them
like chattel slaves the agony of feeding them abstract theories they do not
understand
t he agony of their lugubrious eyes and bartered souls the agony of giving them
party cards but never party support
the agony of marshalling them on election day but never on banquet nights
the agony of giving them mellifluous words but mildewed bread
the agony of their cooking hearths dampened with unuse
the agony of their naked feet on the hot burning tarmac
the agony of their children with projectile bellies
the agony of long miserable nights
that agony of their thatched houses with too many holes
the agony of erecting hotels but being barred from them
the agony of watching cavalcade of limousines
the agony of grand state balls for God knows who
the agony of those who study meaningless 'isms in
incomprehensible languages
the agony of intolerable fees for schools but with no jobs in sight
the agony of it all I say the agony of it all
but above all the damn agony of appealing to their patience
Africa beware! their patience is running out!

Myopia

On rainy mornings
you will see them drenched

PEASANTS! shivering in their emaciated bones
along the boulevards of misery

the boulevards of this country
are railway tracks in my heart
a train of anguish runs on them
rage corollary of hunger
the ricepads of this country
are putrid marshlands in my soul
tended by no magic fertilizers

mountain if the wind blows tomorrow
make me a sabre of that wind
if the skeletons of stillborn promises
dry up in the catacombs
make me the incendiary bomb
if madness we must have
let me be the hangman hanging myself
hanging them hanging the day
not by its neck not by its belly
but by its heart seen in its great betrayal!

Iyamide Hazeley

Born on 21 July, 1957 in Freetown, Sierra Leone, she spent her formative years there. She holds a BA Honours in Social Science, a Postgraduate Certificate in Education, and an MA in Education in Developing Countries.
Iyamide Hazeley's first published work (short stories) appeared in *West Africa* magazine. She has since published poetry in several anthologies.
     In 1983, she received a Minority Rights Group/MAAS Award for her poetry. Presently, Iyamide Hazeley writes more of fiction than poetry.

Beloved

I brought my love
wrapped
in cottons and silks
its face and -hands
washed
clean as an innocent.
I cupped my hands
for love to drink from,
filled,
filled
with the sweet
mingling
of joy with fear.
I bared the red,
soft,
centre
where my heart had been
to nourish my beloved
and turn the hunger inside
into a field in harvest

My love was tumbled to the ground
doused with the salt from my own eyes
then tossed aside in a careless gesture.

He who cannot accept a gift of love
does not deserve it.

Playing our Song

You came in
through a chink in my armour
mouthing tender, playful things
to allay my fears,
occupied an instant in our lives
and turned away.

A solitary note
chimed in the small of my back
The clock struck
a spirit passed
and you were gone.

Lungi Crossing

Early in the morning
after sixteen years away
with still one leg of the journey
remaining,
I arrived home.

The air, the water, the sky
all were tinged
with the blue
of early morning
darkness.

Slowly,
the ferry's motion
through the water,
nudged the sun
into the sky.

I leant one foot
and one elbow
against the rails,

watched as children
and grown people
milled about
squeezing past cars
parked cheek by jowl
on the deck.

There we all werc.
Those coming
to visit ageing parents
those who came to meet
those coming to visit
those wearing the affluence
of tourists
those bringing home their dead
and those simply
coming home.

For Michael Smith
(14 Sept. 1954 - 17 Aug. 1983)

Jamaica
of Maroon-resistance-gun and struggle

In my country too
Anyone can become president
but not an alien

In the land of "truth" and "justice"
our people fought not to die on welfare

In my country too
Sergeant Majors grow fat
in seat of office

In my country too
missiles are hurled
at the heads of the dispossessed

In my country too
they fill mouths with silence
of the silent majority

If poets could be stifled
the whole world would choke
on the words muffled in their throats

But we have our poets-our griots-
the captive minds unfurl

the silence now erupts
in quiet mumbling corners
the voices join our own
join with others
rise and rise
encircle and begin again
that same breath which gave life to thought
inspires

Lemuel Johnson

Born in Northern Nigeria of Sierra Leonean parents, Lemuel Johnson has taught at Fourah Bay College of the University of Sierra Leone. Presently, he is a professor at the University of Michigan.

He has published a book of literary criticism, The *Devil, the Gargoyle and the Buffoon: the Negro as Metaphor in Western Literature.* His short stories and critical articles have appeared in several journals such as *The Literary Review* and *African Writing Today.* Among his books of poetry are *Highlife for Caliban* and *Hand on the Navel.*

Robben Island
(after Sheik Amidou Kane)

civilization is after all merely
the architecture of our response to history:

before the earth understood
what Copernicus knew it stood
still while, for instance,
men at Sodom or Gomorrah
put delicate mouths to each other
and licked off fires

while, for instance,
somebody's wife cracked into salt
and the seventh frequencies of horns
cracked the walls of this or that city

for those of us
fashioned,
to live on the backs of others
the exaltation of ram
horns holds few testaments

On Robben Island, for instance,
shy wardens have been known
to look away
while urinating into the mouth
and scattered teeth of prisoners.

al-Mukhlit*

there are those of us who,
having shaved the insides of
our nostrils and ears, sit down
to food for which
there exists no known botanical names

for a mithkal**
we pushed rotten logs
where the river
coughed in a dry season

the upper reaches
of the river curve away
from long-jointed minarets
the scales of fresh-water fish are in our clean nostrils

here, Djenne*** smells like a drowned lake
there are dead fishes among the roots of bamboo trees
the red eyes of hungry lepers search among broken pots
for the crooked necks of partridges.

there are no deltas in the plains
but leeches reach the head waters:
ochre-coloured lithams dry out the heads of the mixers
the muezzin leans over the dead stones of the river

in december the harmattan blows cold sand
our grey fingers keep warm inside the grey bellies of fish
there are small scales floating to the deltas
on the thin red entrails of the dead.

*al-Mukhlit: the mixers; i.e. heretics, apostates.
**Mithkal is a unit of measurement especially of precious metals such as gold.
***Djenne is an ancient city in present day Mali which was a pro- sperous and flourishing centre of trade in the 15th Century.

Jonathan A. Peters

Born on 3 August, 1943 in Freetown, Sierra Leone, he did his high schooling there at the Methodist Boys' High School and then read English for undergraduate work at Fourah Bay College, also in Freetown. He continued his graduate work at the University of Alberta in Canada where he received the MA and the PhD.

Jonathan Peters has travelled widely in Africa, Europe and the United States and has taught at Albert Academy in Freetown, the University of Alberta, the City University of New York's La Guardia Community College, and is presently teaching at the University of Maryland-Baltimore County.

In addition to his many critical articles and reviews, he has published a major book of literary criticism titled, *A Dance of Masks: Senghor, Achebe, Soyinka*. *He* is presently completing two books - much focusing on and analysing the works of the Senegalese novelist and film-maker Sembene Ousmane.

breast feeding

I have been crying, inconsolable
For the milk from your breasts
Do not give me water from the bottle
For no comforter will appease me
No food strained sieve
And milk of goat or cow,
Let me feed on your milk
The right breast first, knowledge;
Then the left breast, for insight,
Oh, I am ravenous tonight.
Such mortal longings chase me now
Feed my hunger and make me strong
Tomorrow comes when I must leave,
My father's business beckoning me.

Integer

No lottery
this

Trucking with *Eshu*
To make a
windfall

No assembly-line
either
Fitting prefab parts
one to the
other

Empirical process?
never
Unless you can collect
Wind in a
sieve

No nuclear fission
can
Make this a proper
Or improper
fraction

Yet this equation
still
Has its own
Which any can follow
guided

Don't look to
see
With naked eye
The cargo
poised

The rockets
fired
Tracked through mind
Giving periodic
boosters

Speed steadily on
toward
The omega point
Of no return
earthwards

To reach
the
Pure payload
Spirit fragment
whole

Kwame Cumale Fitzjohn

Born on 10 May 1955 in Freetown, Sierra Leone, Kwame Fitzjohn did his under-graduate studies in English and History at Fourah Bay College, Sierra Leone. He did further training in journalism and presently works as a Washington correspondent for the British Broadcasting Corporation (BBC) World Service for Africa.

Kwame Fitzjohn has written feature articles, broadcast, and conducted interviews with several international stars and/or world leaders. He is a former Vice-President of the Sierra Leonean Association of Writers and Illustrators, and has acted in George Wolfe's play, *Return to Glutten*, held at the New Federal Theatre of New York.

The Changing Hour

For my people this Song is sung

my people with the yellow pan-lamps under bamboo roofs

stupor in their minds, fusing with the darkness of darkest night

to be refreshed in the light of coming day

my people with backs bent under the sun

Severe dearth mushrooming in the land

Manifestly, express on their faces "the guest"

as to the whys and hows—and when...!

The time has drawn nigh

And it is Now the answers must unravel

From the maze

"The wheel is come full circle"

Rendering interpretation of the language of the soul

And in the changing hour

the song of my people can hold no more

it bursts forth as NEW BLOOD

piercing through the cells of man

revivifying, revitalizing, reverberating

splurging, spurting, sputtering

gushing forth in the spirit of the Bunbuna Falls*

we are surging in shore.

For in the changing hour

the last minute is struck

the second dies out

changing times flit away

the hour changes no more

it has run its course

the fields pause for a breath-take...

*Bunbuna Falls.- waterfalls in Sierra Leone.

Togo

Gnoussira. Dogbe.

Analla Gnoussira

Born on 7 November, 1954 in Northern Togo. He did his undergraduate studies (i.e., Licence) at the Université du Benin, Lomé, in English Language. He later continued his studies at Colchester English Study Centre in Britain where he received an Education diploma in the Teaching of English as a Foreign Language (TEFL). He has since received his MA (Education) in Language and Linguistics. Analla Gnoussira has taught at Lycée de Pya, Kara, Togo and, worked in various educational capacities in his home-country.

He has published a book of poems, *Morte Saison,* in the Nouvelles Editions Africaines series. His poems have also been featured in a small anthology edited by Jean-Francois Brierre and in several. issues of the monthly *Poet International (India).*

Gerlinde

There are a thousand auras in your sun-charmer look
and I who tamed you at the sole mention of your name,
I wonder if I ever knew you.

A thousand thoughts buzz in your eyes
like a heat-plague.
The green tranquillity of your voice
implores the passion of Christ
while angels across the faith
cheer your moral.
Was it ever known what exoticism
Irrigated your blood in a trance,
you mute shepherdess?

In the troubled waters of conscience,
remorse imposes on us
The delirium of loss
and quietly the memory
of a posthumous encounter schematically
takes shape. In your ashen look,

the barriers surpass themselves in vain.

You are a painting
that irritates judgment ,
through its absence.

Or may be inflation that defeats hope.
All the eyes carry you—rape of the mind--
while my recollection of you, tired
of resisting,
gives up

Dear Guerrelasse!

Mind On A Rocker

If I was gifted at painting, I would be
A "neantist," drawing empty bellies
and ghostly rumours from moods of air.
But I am not a painter, not even a poet.
I do not want to have anything
To do with Beauty Queens. Designing faces
Is not an easy affair.
I know what I am talking about.

Now, I go swallowing all the baobab seeds
in the world. Or I may stand by and watch
my stomach wrestling with vomits of yesterday.

The custom says, we should insult
our Brother-in-law when unhappiness enters
the family; I know it only too well.
I even open my eyes in the morning
To see the sun rise. It leaves me wondering what
fate might drop in my mouth; the last image
of my shadow or someone's cherished sister... ?

You, Arssie, do winds blow in your country?
However strong, Assane*, they have not stolen
your soul. Only your songs. And who cares
when the song-tree is not uprooted?

*Arssie and Assane- a reference to the same person.

Harmattan*

Unusual day, isn't it?
Looks like the end of the world:
The sun, half-dead;
Life calcining in the lazy morning fire...
That's the harmattan.

It's a natural law to laugh
But here, no tooth to be seen!
Time improvises fashion-faces
With new look for lips
With dry noses
And plenty of mentholatum...
That's the harmattan.

In the black country
Everyone has whitened
Only the hair makes the difference,
Hidden under a cap, or
headgear. Everything looks
so severe...
That's the harmattan.

* Harmattan: A cool, dry wind that blows across West Africa from around December to
March

Yves-Emmanuel Dogbe

Born on 10 May, 1939 in Lomé, Togo. He studied Philosophy and Sociology at Sorbonne in Paris, and was a student at l'Ecole des Hautes Etudes en Sciences Sociales. He holds the *Docteur de Troisième Cycle,* and was a professor at Togo. Dogbe was detained in his home country for an article titled "Black Civilization and the Future of Africa" prepared for the Festival of Negro Arts and Culture held in Lagos, Nigeria. He presently lives in Paris.

Among his many works are two novels, *La Victime* and *L'Incarcéré,* and an anthology of poems from Togo titled *Anthologie de la poesie togolaise.*

Derceto
(Daniel H.)

I climbed the mount of
Las Mercedes
Where the clouds are formed
And watched them stream
Up and down the valley
Of the isles called Canaries

Droplets swarmed around
My face when I thought of YOU
Derceto, Sybil of the sea

The breeze blows wispy strands
of white hair across your
Aquatic eyes
As you whisper secrets
Of the first volcano
To emerge from the lost
Continent of Atlantis

Each gesture a parthenon frieze
Lasting as long as the flying
Fish spreads its finny wings
Before the final plunge

Datsa

Datsa!
I remember...
I remember the good deeds I did in your crooked
world when more and more you choked up my groove
and squeezed it to blood.

I remember the bad things I performed under your
burning eyes the flames of which are consuming my
mind now that I have become your breath.

I must vomit out all the disgusting wind you stocked
in my heart for fear I get ecstasized and drag you out
necked before men.

I know you once loved me...

Isn't it love when by the time birds started chattering
on the wings of decayed palm-trees you led me by the
hand over the heaven of your silly hills?

Isn't it love when the sun swelling and becoming bigger
and bigger and fire and full of fun in the horizon
you blew me out on your twisted entrails?

I sailed my sorrowful soul amidst the perverted flowers
of your womanhood who smiled to him as secretly
as life smiles to youth.

Why didn't you let me suck for a long time the sweet
substance of your scent?

Why did you obturate my throat and blind him from
hearing in order to know?

O Datsa! Who then can loan me new wings to fly
back like a dove to your dishonest bosom where vile
deeds are done?

Remember

When the night arrives
Dragging along its black veil
When breeze pours forth, fresh,
Smooth and sweet as the flight of a swallow
When shadow falls and covers every thing
That breathes
When stars appear gay and full of life
Twinkling in the depth of the sky
And when nature calls every soul to rest
From the incessant weariness of man
Remember, ô Africa my only love
I still think of you